# I'm A Christian

## Now What? Vol. 2

### The Life of Jesus

TODD CAPPS AND CAROL ELLIS
CONTRIBUTING EDITORS

| | | |
|---|---|---|
| GORDON BROWN | JEFF LAND | WILLIAM SUMMEY |
| HENRY DUTTON | TIM POLLARD | RHONDA VANCLEAVE. |
| BILL EMEOTT | TRACEY ROGERS | JERRY VOGEL |
| LANDRY HOLMES | KLISTA STORTS | |

LifeWay Press®
Nashville, TN 37234

ISBN: 9781430025580
Item #: 005592093
Dewey: 242.62
SUBHD: DEVOTIONAL LITERATURE FOR CHILDREN \ CHRISTIAN LIFE \ JESUS CHRIST

Printed in the United States of America.

Kids Ministry Publishing
LifeWay Church Resources
One LifeWay Plaza
Nashville, Tennessee 37234-0172

We believe the Bible has God for its author; salvation for its end;
and truth, without any mixture of error, for its matter
and that all Scripture is totally true and trustworthy.
To review LifeWay's doctrinal guideline
Please visit *www.lifeway.com/doctrinalguideline.*

# TABLE OF CONTENTS

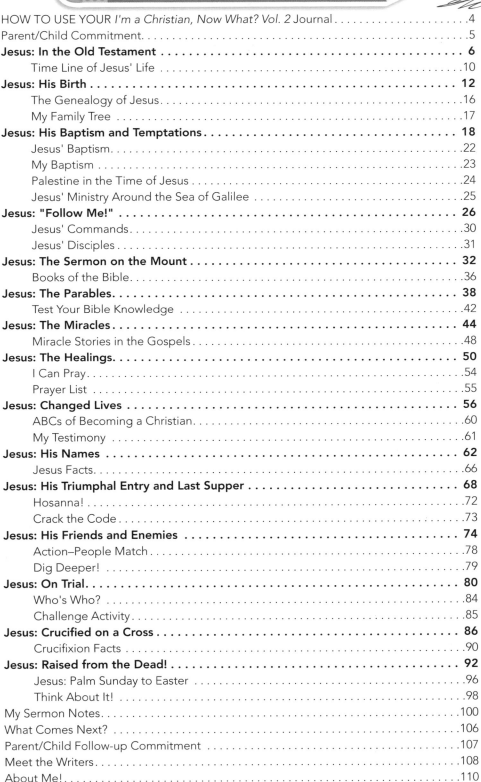

# HOW TO USE YOUR
## I'M A CHRISTIAN, NOW WHAT? VOL. 2 JOURNAL

Asking Jesus to be your Savior and Lord is the most important decision you will ever make. No one can take that decision away from you. Now that you are a Christian, it is important to learn more about Jesus. That's the purpose of this journal. The information on these pages will help you discover more about the life of Jesus and what He expects of you as one of His followers. Here are some tips on how to use your journal.

- ✓ Ask your parents to read page 5 with you. After reading the promises, you and your parents should sign the pledges.
- ✓ Begin with the introduction to the first set of devotions (page 6). Read the introduction and the Day 1 devotion. Only complete one day's activities at a time.
- ✓ Locate the "Verse(s) of the Day" in your Bible. Take a few minutes to read and think about the verse(s).
- ✓ Challenge yourself to read additional verses by locating, reading, and thinking about the "Challenge" verse(s).
- ✓ Make notes, write, and draw in your journal! This is *your* journal, so take notes about what you discover and how God speaks to you.

- ✓ Listen for God to speak to you each day.
- ✓ Keep your journal in a safe place.
- ✓ Start again (where you stopped) if you miss a day.
- ✓ Ask your parents (or another adult) to help you if you do not understand something.
- ✓ Follow the prayer suggestions each day. Listen to what God says to you.
- ✓ Take as long as you need each day to finish the activities.
- ✓ Pay attention to what you read. As you work through your journal, you may think you have read some of the information in a previous study. That's right! Some of the information about the life of Jesus relates to more than one week's study and is included more than one time.

Included in your journal are some pages your parents will work on with you. When you see "Parent Page Alert!" take your journal to your parents and ask them to do the activity with you.

# PARENT/CHILD COMMITMENT

Dear Parents,

Your child has made the most important decision he will ever make. His decision to ask Jesus to be his Savior and Lord is one that not only affects his life now, but for eternity. God instructs you—parents—to teach your child (Deuteronomy 6:4-9). This *I'm a Christian, Now What? Vol. 2* journal is designed to help your child grow in his knowledge and understanding of Jesus. Each week, your child will explore a new topic related to the life of Jesus and have six daily devotions to complete. If possible, begin on Monday with the introduction and Day 1 devotion. No devotions are included for Sundays, so use this as a time to worship with your child.

Encourage your child to complete as much of the journal as possible on his own. Allow him to learn how to use his Bible, respond to questions, and pray. Be available and ready to help when he needs assistance. One of the most important things you can do is pray for your child on a daily basis.

Ready to get started? Read the pledges below with your child. Take a few minutes to pray together, then sign the pledges.

## PARENT AND CHILD PLEDGES

### PARENT'S PLEDGE

✓ I promise to pray for and encourage you each day.
✓ I promise to help you when you need help.
✓ I promise not to read your journal unless you give me permission.

Signed *Melanie Lipsword*

Date *8-10-16*

### CHILD'S PLEDGE

✓ I promise to pray for myself each day.
✓ I promise to ask for help when I need help.
✓ I promise to make it a priority to complete my devotion each day.

Signed *mackenzee Lipsword*

Date *8-10-16*

# JESUS: IN THE OLD TESTAMENT

LANDRY HOLMES

If a friend were to ask you to describe the Old Testament, what would you say? Would you tell your friend the Old Testament is the first part of the Bible? Would you say the Old Testament has 39 individual books? Perhaps you might mention the Old Testament has five divisions: Law, History, Poetry, Major Prophets, and Minor Prophets. You might even answer that the Old Testament tells us about things that happened before Jesus was born.

Next, your friend could ask you to describe the New Testament. Would you state that the New Testament tells about Jesus' birth, life, death, and resurrection? You might even say the New Testament tells about the beginning of the church. And, you could say there are 27 books in the New Testament, and five divisions: Gospels, History, Paul's Letters, General Letters, and Prophecy.

All of your answers would be correct, but not completely true. The whole Bible, both the Old and New Testaments, is actually ONE story. The entire Bible—all 66 books and all 10 divisions—is God's story.

Since the Bible is God's story, then both the Old and New Testaments tell about God's Son, Jesus. While the name *Jesus* is not found in the Old Testament, other names for Jesus are. We will discover one of those names this week.

In the New Testament, Paul reminds us Jesus has existed since before the beginning of the world. Not only has Jesus always existed, He created the world. Think about that for a moment. Jesus is Creator, just as God the Father is Creator. Jesus did not appear 2,000 years after God created the earth. Jesus has always been present, even before the earth came into existence.

The New Testament is not the only place we learn about Jesus and the proof of His existence. The prophets in the Old Testament told about One who would come to earth to rescue God's people from sin. Over and over, Old Testament prophets proclaimed the coming of a Messiah. However, before the prophets told about Jesus, God said in the first book of the Bible that He would send a Savior into the world (see Genesis 3:15—you will learn more about this verse on Day 2).

Why is a Savior needed? Why did Jesus need to leave heaven and come to earth as a baby? Why did Jesus need to grow up and become a man? Why did Jesus need to die? Why did God raise Jesus from the dead? Why is Jesus alive today?

As you read and study the Bible over the next 15 weeks, you'll begin to discover the answers to these questions. Just remember that the entire Bible is ONE story—God's story. That story tells us about Jesus and how we should live as Christians.

# DAY 1

## JESUS HAS ALWAYS BEEN

VERSES OF THE DAY: John 1:1-3
CHALLENGE: John 1:1-18

**DO!** Write your answers to these questions.

 How do you know if something or someone is real?

*I belive*

How do you know Jesus is real? *Becasue*

*He save us for our Sins*

What would you tell a friend who asked you to prove Jesus is real and has always existed?

*No*

**KNOW!**

✓ Jesus was with God since the beginning of time. Jesus is God (John 1:1-2).
✓ Jesus created the world (Colossians 1:15-17).
✓ Jesus is fully God and when He came to earth, Jesus was fully man too (Philippians 2:5-11).
✓ Jesus is God's Son (Galatians 4:4).
✓ A lot of people in the New Testament did not recognize Jesus as God's Son (John 1:10).
✓ Many people today still don't believe that Jesus is God's Son.

**PRAY** Thank God for His Son, Jesus. Tell God you believe Jesus has always existed. Ask God to help you tell someone about Jesus this week.

---

# DAY 2

## GOD'S PLAN FROM THE BEGINNING WAS JESUS

VERSES OF THE DAY: Genesis 3:14-15
CHALLENGE: Genesis 3:1-24

**DO!** The story in Genesis 3 is real and true, and much more exciting than what we find in comic books. In the spaces below, draw your own pictures showing what Genesis 3:14 and 3:17-18 say will happen as a result of Adam and Eve's sin.

GENESIS 3:14

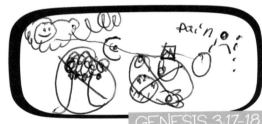

GENESIS 3:17-18

**KNOW!**

✓ God knows everything! He knew Adam and Eve would sin by disobeying Him.
✓ But, God had a plan to deal with sin. That plan was, and still is, Jesus.
✓ Jesus came to earth so He could die for our sins and be raised from the dead.
✓ Jesus is alive!
✓ Jesus defeated Satan, just as God said He would (Genesis 3:15).

**PRAY** Thank God that Jesus died for your sins and He rose from the dead to give you eternal life. Ask God to help you not sin.

# THE OLD TESTAMENT TELLS ABOUT GOD'S PLAN

VERSE OF THE DAY: Isaiah 7:14 / CHALLENGE: Matthew 1:18-23

**DO!** A *plan* is "knowing what you want to do in the future." Circle the pictures that represent things you plan to do or places you plan to go.

Do any of these plans include Jesus? Place a check mark by the pictures of plans that include Jesus.

**KNOW!**

✓ *Immanuel* is another name for Jesus. The name means "God with us."
✓ God's plan is to be with us through His Son, Jesus.
✓ After you become a Christian, Jesus is always with you.
✓ Since Jesus is always with you, your plans should always start with Jesus.

**PRAY** Thank God that He is always with you through His Son, Jesus. Ask God to help you always include Jesus first in your plans.

# THE OLD TESTAMENT TELLS ABOUT JESUS' BIRTH

VERSE OF THE DAY: Micah 5:2 / CHALLENGE: Matthew 2:1-12

**DO!** Ask your mom or dad to help you answer these questions about where you were born:

## MY BIRTHPLACE

What city/town were you born in? _____

What state were you born in? _____

What country were you born in? _____

If you were born in a hospital, what is the hospital's name?

_____

If you weren't born in a hospital, where were you born?

_____

**KNOW!**

✓ Jesus' earthly ancestors (older family members) included Abraham, Ruth, Boaz, and King David.
✓ Ruth and Boaz lived in Bethlehem, a town near Jerusalem. David was anointed king in Bethlehem too.
✓ About 700 years before Jesus was born, the prophet Micah said Jesus would be born in Bethlehem.
✓ *Bethlehem* means "house of bread."

**PRAY** Thank God that He loves you so much He kept His promise to send His Son, Jesus, to be born in a small town.

## DAY 5

### THE OLD TESTAMENT TELLS ABOUT JESUS' WORK

VERSES OF THE DAY: Isaiah 61:1-3
CHALLENGE: Luke 4:16-21

**DO!** Jesus wants the church to continue the work He started 2,000 years ago. As a kid, you are not too young to help your church do that work. Draw a smiley face by the things listed below that you can help your church do.

____ Feed hungry people

____ Give money to help missionaries

____ Clean flower beds for an older adult

____ Tell your friends about Jesus and how they can become Christians

____ Invite your friends to church

____ Other:

**KNOW!**

✓ The tradition Jesus followed was to read from what we know as part of the Old Testament. Then, Jesus explained what the Scripture passage meant.
✓ Jesus read a prophecy from the Book of Isaiah that was about the Messiah.
✓ The prophet Isaiah told what the Messiah would do when He came to earth.
✓ Jesus told the people that Isaiah was talking about Him. Jesus is the Messiah.

**PRAY** Thank God for the work Jesus came to do. Ask God to help you do the things He wants you to do.

## DAY 6

### THE OLD TESTAMENT TELLS ABOUT JESUS' DEATH AND RESURRECTION!

VERSES OF THE DAY: Psalm 16:8-11; Isaiah 53:4-6
CHALLENGE: Acts 2:22-36; 8:26-40

**DO!** This week you learned that all of the Bible—the Old and New Testaments—tells you about Jesus. The Bible tells us why Jesus came to earth, why He had to die, and how He rose from the dead. The Bible also helps you know how Christians can do the things Jesus wants them to do.

Look back at each of this week's devotions. Write down one fact or thought from each of the past six days that you want to remember.

DAY 1 _____
DAY 2 _____
DAY 3 _____
DAY 4 _____
DAY 5 _____
TODAY _____

**KNOW!**

✓ The prophet Isaiah wrote the Messiah would suffer and die for our sins.
✓ King David wrote about the promise of the Messiah's resurrection from the dead.
✓ Peter preached about Jesus' death and resurrection.
✓ Philip used Scripture from Isaiah to tell an Ethiopian man about Jesus.

**PRAY** Thank God for His Son, Jesus. Thank Him for giving you the Bible that tells you about Jesus. Ask God to help you remember what He has taught you this week.

# TIME LINE OF JESUS' LIFE

**1** Born in Bethlehem

**2** Worshiped by the shepherds

**3** Greeted by Simeon and Anna in the temple

**9** Preached the Sermon on the Mount

**11** Healed Jairus' daughter

**10** Calmed a storm

**12** Fed the 5,000

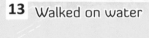

**13** Walked on water

**14** Healed 10 men with skin disease

**22** Buried in a tomb

**21** Crucified on a cross

**23** Resurrected: Jesus is alive!

**24** Appeared to many people

**4** Visited by the wise men

**5**

Learned at
the temple

**6** Baptized by John

**8**

Called the
first disciples

**7**

Tempted by
the Devil

**15** Blessed the children

**16**

Visited
Zacchaeus

**17**

Entered Jerusalem triumphantly

**20**

Arrested
and tried

**19**

Prayed in
Gethsemane

**18**

Had the Last Supper
with the disciples

**25**

Cooked breakfast
for disciples

**26** Ascended to heaven

# JESUS: HIS BIRTH

JERRY VOGEL

The birth of Jesus is exciting in many ways! Just think, God sent Jesus to earth just for us! God loves us so much that He knew we needed a way for our sins to be forgiven. His plan to send Jesus wasn't so we could have a holiday, give and receive gifts, or have a birthday party. God sent Jesus to us so He could teach us about God's love, die on the cross for our sins, and live forever as the Savior of the world.

As we celebrate the birth of Jesus each year at Christmas, we have opportunities to not only think about what Jesus came to earth to do, but to tell the whole world about the real reason God sent Jesus. Many people are more interested in hearing about Jesus at Christmastime than at other times. The story of Jesus' birth can be the starting place to tell people about Jesus.

Was Jesus really born on December 25? Possibly not. The details in the Bible about Jesus' birth—and about other people and events surrounding His birth—lead many people to believe Jesus, the Messiah, was born around late 5 B.C.—early 4 B.C., and possibly between November and March. But guess what? The actual day and year of Jesus' birth are not the most important things to know. What is important is that the stories in the Bible about God sending Jesus as a baby are true. Jesus grew up to be a boy, and then a man who did things that no one else could do—especially dying on a cross for our sins. Now that's something to celebrate!

During the next six days, you will have opportunities to study the details of Jesus' birth. Challenge yourself to read these Bible verses and thoughts as if you were hearing them for the very first time (which maybe you are!). As you read and study, remember that these stories are about real people who lived on this earth just like you. Every detail of Jesus' birth is important and worth learning about. God wants you to see that He has taken care of exactly what needs to be done for each of us to become part of God's forever family.

## DAY 1

# MARY AND JOSEPH HEAR FROM ANGELS

VERSES OF THE DAY: Luke 1:30-31; Matthew 1:20-21 / CHALLENGE: Luke 1:26-38; Matthew 1:18-21

**DO!** Ask your mom or dad what it was like when they found out you were going to be born. Did an angel speak to them? Did a doctor help them understand that you were "on the way"?

Put these details about the birth of Jesus in the right order by numbering the events *1-5*. Read Luke 1:26-38 if you need help.

____ Mary said, "I am the Lord's servant; let it be as you say."
____ The angel Gabriel told Mary that she would have a son.
____ Mary was confused and worried about this sudden news, but she had faith in God.
____ The angel Gabriel appeared to a young Jewish woman named Mary.
____ Mary was told to name the baby Jesus and He would be the Son of God.

 **KNOW!**

✓ God chose Mary and Joseph to be Jesus' parents here on earth.
✓ God gave Mary and Joseph only the details and information they needed at that moment.
✓ Mary and Joseph obeyed God and were willing to be part of His plan.
✓ God planned for Jesus from the beginning of time.

**PRAY** Thank God for sending Jesus as a baby. Ask Him if there are areas in your life where you need to obey Him.

## DAY 2

# THE TRIP TO BETHLEHEM

VERSES OF THE DAY: Luke 2:1-4 / CHALLENGE: Matthew 1:1-17

**DO!** Think about these things:
? Do you think the trip from Nazareth to Bethlehem was an easy one? ☐ yes ☐ no
? Do you think Mary and Joseph understood everything about God's plan? ☐ yes ☐ no
? Has God ever asked you to do something that was not easy? ☐ yes ☐ no

Draw a face showing how you felt when God led you to do something you didn't understand.

 **KNOW!**

✓ Mary and Joseph lived in a town called Nazareth (NAZ uh reth).
✓ Mary and Joseph had to travel to Bethlehem, where Joseph's family was from, in order to register to pay their taxes.
✓ Both Nazareth and Bethlehem were in the country now called Israel.
✓ The trip to Bethlehem was about 65-70 miles from Nazareth.

**PRAY** Thank God for working in the lives of Mary and Joseph so Jesus would be born exactly where the Bible said He would. Tell God you love Him for keeping His promise.

## DAY 3 — THE PLACE JESUS WAS BORN

VERSES OF THE DAY: Luke 2:6-7
CHALLENGE: Luke 2:1-5

 **DO!** Think about these things: Have you ever stayed in a hotel? What was it like? If you haven't stayed in a hotel, what do you think it would be like?

❓ How does it make you feel to know that God's Son, Jesus, was born in a stable?

❓ In the space below, draw a picture of what you think the stable where Jesus was born might have looked like. Draw a manger that would have been Jesus' bed.

 **KNOW!**

✓ When Mary and Joseph got to Bethlehem, there was no place for them to stay because the inns (hotels) were already full.

✓ Mary and Joseph stayed in a stable, a place where animals were kept, and probably used fresh hay for beds.

✓ The stable didn't have a baby crib, so Mary and Joseph laid Jesus in a manger (a feeding box for animals). The manger probably had fresh hay in it to make a soft bed.

**PRAY** Thank God for your family. Thank Him for giving you a family who can take care of you. Thank Him for where you live and all of the wonderful things you enjoy.

## DAY 4 — THE SHEPHERDS WORSHIP

VERSES OF THE DAY: Luke 2:15-20
CHALLENGE: Luke 2:1-20

**DO!** Think about what it means to worship God and Jesus. Worship involves telling God you love Him and thanking Him for loving you.

The shepherds found Baby Jesus in the manger and worshiped Him. Find these "ways to worship" words in the puzzle: pray, sing, read Bible, obey, give, serve, share faith, be thankful, love others, use talents.

```
E X K G C B R G H S L U
J V A X D Q N N T Z R S
S V R K B I N K I E L E
S E J E S S U H A U B T
P Y G R S S N D F C L A
T A S C J O B K E M I L
C R G E I I N G R P W E
Z P E L B A U B A S B N
R S G L H Z J O H E A T
Y R E T G I V E S H P S
X B E R D D O G Y E B O
M B L O V E O T H E R S
```

What are some other ways you can worship Jesus?

 **KNOW!**

✓ After an angel told some shepherds the Messiah had been born in Bethlehem, they found Jesus in a manger and worshiped Him.

✓ The shepherds told everyone they could about the good news of Jesus' birth.

✓ God wants us to tell people about Jesus.

**PRAY** Tell God how much you love Him. Thank Him for all He has done for you. Thank Him for specific things: your family, church, Jesus, and your salvation.

# DAY 5

## THE WISE MEN VISIT

VERSES OF THE DAY: Matthew 2:1-2 / CHALLENGE: Matthew 2:3-12

 The wise men brought gifts to Jesus. What gifts can you give to Jesus? Follow the path below. On each box, write one gift you can give to Jesus.

START

FINISH

 **KNOW!**

✓ Wise men from eastern countries saw a star in the sky and followed it to find Jesus.

✓ The wise men brought Jesus gold, frankincense, and myrrh—some of the finest things in the world at that time.

✓ God helped the wise men know not to tell King Herod where Jesus was because Herod wanted to hurt or kill Jesus.

**PRAY** Thank God for helping you know about Jesus and His birth. Ask God how you can show His love to others.

# DAY 6

## GOD'S PLAN FOR ALL

VERSE OF THE DAY: John 3:16 / CHALLENGE: Galatians 4:4; Philippians 2:5-11

 Color in all the 1s in the grid below to reveal a special name.

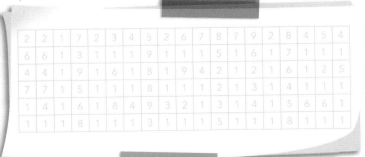

| 2 | 2 | 1 | 7 | 2 | 3 | 4 | 5 | 2 | 6 | 7 | 8 | 7 | 9 | 2 | 8 | 4 | 5 | 4 |
| 6 | 6 | 1 | 3 | 1 | 1 | 1 | 9 | 1 | 1 | 1 | 5 | 1 | 6 | 1 | 7 | 1 | 1 | 1 |
| 4 | 4 | 1 | 9 | 1 | 6 | 1 | 8 | 1 | 9 | 4 | 2 | 1 | 2 | 1 | 6 | 1 | 2 | 5 |
| 7 | 7 | 1 | 5 | 1 | 1 | 1 | 8 | 1 | 1 | 1 | 2 | 1 | 3 | 1 | 4 | 1 | 1 | 1 |
| 1 | 4 | 1 | 6 | 1 | 8 | 4 | 9 | 3 | 2 | 1 | 3 | 1 | 4 | 1 | 5 | 6 | 6 | 1 |
| 1 | 1 | 1 | 8 | 1 | 1 | 1 | 3 | 1 | 1 | 1 | 5 | 1 | 1 | 1 | 8 | 1 | 1 | 1 |

What special name did you discover?

Think about Christmas and Easter. Why do we celebrate Christmas and Easter?

 **KNOW!**

✓ We have all sinned (chosen our way instead of God's way).

✓ We need a Savior who can save us from our sins.

✓ Jesus is God's Son and our Savior. Jesus died on the cross for our sins.

✓ If we ask, our sins will be forgiven.

✓ We can become part of God's family and go to heaven and live with Him forever.

**PRAY** Thank God for sending Jesus to be your Savior. Ask Him to help you tell others about Jesus.

# THE GENEALOGY OF JESUS

A *genealogy* is "a study of a person's line of ancestors (people in his family)." Read Matthew 1:1-16 and fill in the blanks with the missing names to learn about Jesus' genealogy.
(NOTE: Some Bible translations spell the names differently.)

### From Abraham to David

_____ fathered Isaac,
Isaac fathered Jacob,
Jacob fathered _____,
_____ fathered Perez,
Perez fathered Hezron,
Hezron fathered _____,
_____ fathered Amminadab,
Amminadab fathered Nahshon,
Nahshon fathered Salmon,
Salmon fathered _____,
_____ fathered Obed,
Obed fathered Jesse,
and Jesse fathered _____.

### From David to the Babylonian Exile

_____ fathered Solomon,
Solomon fathered Rehoboam,
Rehoboam fathered Abijah,
Abijah fathered _____,
_____ fathered Jehoshaphat,
Jehoshaphat fathered Joram,
Joram fathered _____,
_____ fathered Jotham,
Jotham fathered Ahaz,
Ahaz fathered Hezekiah,
Hezekiah fathered _____,
_____ fathered Amon,
Amon fathered Josiah,
and Josiah fathered Jechoniah.

### From the Exile to the Messiah

Jechoniah fathered _____,
_____ fathered Zerubbabel,
Zerubbabel fathered Abiud,
Abiud fathered Eliakim,
Eliakim fathered _____,
_____ fathered Zadok,
Zadok fathered Achim,
Achim fathered Eliud,
Eliud fathered _____,
_____ fathered Matthan,
Matthan fathered Jacob, and Jacob fathered
_____ the husband of _____, who gave birth to
_____ who is called the Messiah.

# MY FAMILY TREE

**PARENT PAGE ALERT!**
Enlist your parents' help to complete as much of your family tree (your genealogy) as you can. Ask your parents to share stories about family members as you add their names to the tree.

Do you know who your ancestors are? Start by filling in the box at the bottom of the tree with your name, then add your parents' names and their parents' names (your grandparents). BONUS: Add the names of your grandparents' parents (your great grandparents)!

# JESUS: HIS BAPTISM AND TEMPTATIONS

JEFF LAND

I remember the day I was baptized. I was 6 years old and I wondered what the water would feel like. For some reason, I thought the water was going to be really cold. I got to the big container of water (the baptistry) and dipped my foot in. I was relieved to feel the warm water cover my foot, but I was *not* relieved to see the cricket floating in the water.

Have you ever thought about the day Jesus was baptized in the Jordan River? At our church, we have a baptistry in our sanctuary, but once a year, anyone who would like to be baptized outside can be baptized in a nearby creek. I think the creek is more like what Jesus experienced.

I have not been baptized in a creek, but I have baptized kids in a creek. Guess how it felt? Squishy! I think Jesus probably experienced the same thing. As I baptized kids in the creek, the mud oozed its way up through my toes, and guess what? I even saw a cricket float by—just like when I was baptized in my church's baptistry!

The Bible tells us that John the Baptist baptized Jesus. This week, you will study more about why baptism is so special. You will also learn about how God responded when Jesus was baptized.

After Jesus was baptized, He was tested. These tests were not like math quizzes or spelling tests; they were much more serious. These tests are called *temptations*.

The Devil tempted Jesus. Have you ever been tempted? What tempts you? Read the following list. Would any of these things tempt you?

- Hitting your brother when he makes you mad
- Taking money from your mom's purse when you want to buy a new toy
- Treating someone unkindly because she doesn't look like you
- Talking about someone who dresses different than you
- Eating candy before supper
- Licking your dog

You have probably been tempted to do at least some of the things above. I know I have.

The Bible tells us Jesus was tempted three different ways. This week you will look at the different ways He was tempted and learn how Jesus was able to avoid giving in to temptation.

By following Jesus' example in baptism and by not giving in to temptation, the Holy Spirit will help you to become more like Jesus. Followers of Jesus are supposed to be like Him to the rest of the world.

# DAY 1

## THE WAY OF THE LORD

VERSE OF THE DAY: John 14:6 / CHALLENGE: Matthew 3:1-11

**DO!** Follow the path below. As you reach each obstacle, write one good choice you can make in that situation as you try to become more like Jesus.

What gets in your way when you are trying to be more like Jesus?

**KNOW!**

✓ Sometimes people claim to know another way to heaven, but Jesus is the *only way!*

✓ John the Baptist baptized people who confessed their sins.

✓ God wants people to be baptized after they accept Jesus as their Savior.

**PRAY** Ask God to give you the courage to be baptized. If you have already been baptized, ask Him to help you tell others why baptism is important.

# DAY 2

## JESUS WAS BAPTIZED

VERSE OF THE DAY: Mark 1:9 / CHALLENGE: Matthew 3:13-17

**DO!** Circle the places a person can be baptized:

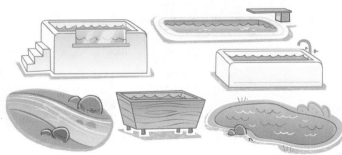

What did you circle? Why?

Can you think of other places a person could be baptized?

**KNOW!**

✓ *Baptize* means "to lower someone in the water and bring him back up."

✓ Jesus "went up from the water" when He was baptized, so we know He was put under the water.

✓ When a person is baptized, she is following Jesus' example.

✓ Baptism does not make a person a Christian, but shows others she has become a Christian.

**PRAY** Thank Jesus for giving you a perfect example to follow. Pray that God will help you be an example to others of how to live like Jesus.

# DAY 3

## JESUS WAS TEMPTED WITH FOOD

VERSE OF THE DAY: Deuteronomy 8:3
CHALLENGE: Matthew 4:1-4

**DO!** Place a check mark by all the things you would eat.

pizza

bread

apple

carrot

CANDY

stones

? What things did you not place a check mark by? Why not?
? Why could you not eat stones?

Jesus had not eaten food for 40 days. The Devil knew Jesus was hungry, so the Devil tempted Jesus to turn the stones into bread. Jesus told the Devil a verse from Deuteronomy that says "man does not live by bread alone."

**KNOW!**

✓ To *tempt* means "to try to get a person to make a wrong choice or action."
✓ God cannot be tempted and He will not tempt anyone.
✓ With the help of the Holy Spirit, you can avoid giving in to temptation.

**PRAY** Ask God to help you avoid giving in to temptation. Thank God for the Holy Spirit who helps His followers when they are tempted.

# DAY 4

## JESUS WAS TEMPTED TO TEST GOD

VERSE OF THE DAY: Deuteronomy 6:16
CHALLENGE: Matthew 4:5-7

**DO!** Did you know you can test your senses? Draw a line from the place on the girl's face to the object that would help test that sense.

? What are some other ways you can test your sense of taste?
? What sense is not listed on the page?
? How can you test your sense of touch?
? How did the Devil tempt Jesus to test God?

**KNOW!**

✓ Temptation comes from the Devil.
✓ The Bible is clear that you should not test God.
✓ If you ask Him, God will forgive you when you give in to temptation.
✓ Memorizing Scripture is a great way to help you avoid giving in to temptation.

**PRAY** Ask God to help you memorize Scripture so you can be prepared to avoid temptation. Thank Him for forgiving you when you mess up.

## DAY 5 — JESUS WAS TEMPTED WITH POWER

VERSE OF THE DAY: Deuteronomy 6:13 / CHALLENGE: Matthew 4:8-11

**DO!** In the box below, draw or write what you would do if you could rule the world.

Ruling the world sure seems like it would be fun! Endless supplies of chocolate ice cream, no bedtime, and ABSOLUTELY no homework! The temptation of power is one that everyone can give in to. Did you know that power can be used to be hurtful? Can you think of examples of when power can be a bad thing?

**KNOW!**
- ✓ God said to worship Him alone.
- ✓ You can avoid temptation by knowing what tempts you and staying away from those things or situations.
- ✓ If you ask Him, God will help you avoid giving in to temptation.

**PRAY** Ask God to help you avoid the temptation of power. Pray that He will help you use your strengths to build others up. Thank God for never leaving you.

## DAY 6 — JESUS OVERCAME TEMPTATION

VERSE OF THE DAY: Philippians 4:13 / CHALLENGE: Proverbs 28:6-10

**DO!** The Bible tells us Jesus used Scripture to help Him when He was tempted. Read the verses and match them to the temptations they might help you avoid.

| When you are tempted to: | Read this: |
|---|---|
| ✓ Talk back to your parents. | Matthew 6:19-21 |
| ✓ Say a bad word. | Proverbs 11:13 |
| ✓ Eat too much. | Ephesians 4:29 |
| ✓ Gossip about a friend. | Proverbs 23:20-21 |
| ✓ Store up money. | Deuteronomy 5:16 |

The Bible is full of Scriptures that will help you know what to do when facing temptation!

**KNOW!** Learn this plan for overcoming temptation:
- ✓ Ask God to help you.
- ✓ Memorize Scripture.
- ✓ Find a person with whom you can talk about the things that tempt you.
- ✓ Admit when you fail and ask God for forgiveness.
- ✓ Avoid places and things you know will tempt you.

**PRAY** Thank God that He always provides protection. Ask God to help you know when you are going to be tempted and how to avoid the temptation.

# JESUS' BAPTISM

Draw a picture of what you think Jesus' baptism looked like.

When Jesus was baptized:

Where Jesus was baptized:

Who baptized Jesus:

Who watched Jesus be baptized:

How do you think Jesus felt after being baptized?

# MY BAPTISM

If you have already been baptized, draw a picture of your baptism.
(Or ask your parents for a picture of your baptism and tape it inside the frame.)

When I was baptized:

Where I was baptized:

Who baptized me:

Who watched me be baptized:

How I felt after being baptized:

# PALESTINE IN THE TIME OF JESUS

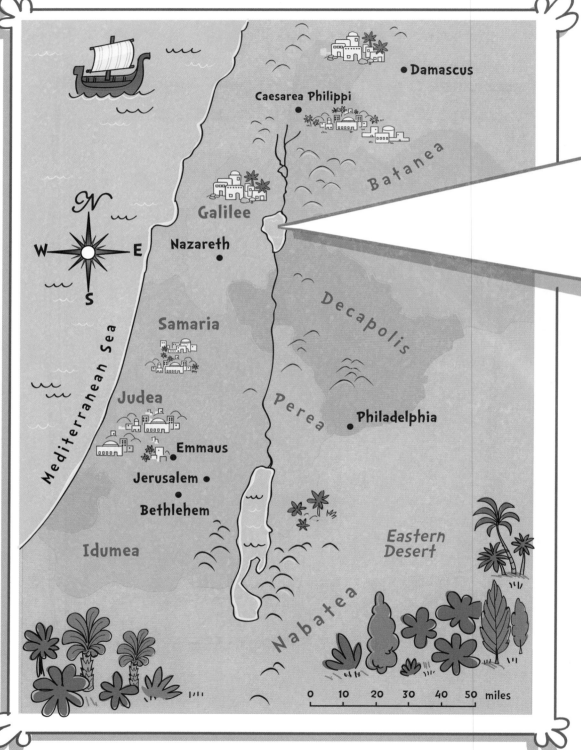

Damascus

Caesarea Philippi

Batanea

Galilee

Nazareth

Decapolis

Samaria

Perea

Judea

Philadelphia

Emmaus

Jerusalem

Bethlehem

Eastern Desert

Idumea

Nabatea

Mediterranean Sea

0  10  20  30  40  50  miles

# JESUS' MINISTRY AROUND THE SEA OF GALILEE

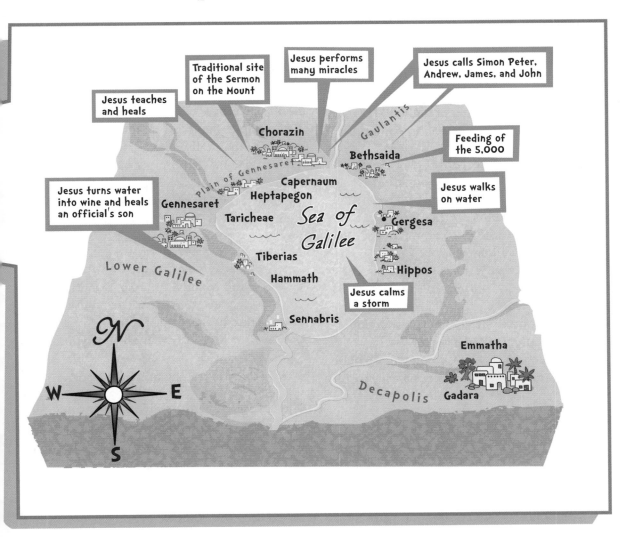

Read the following Bible verses. Write the names of the places mentioned in the verses. Find the places on the maps and touch the names with your finger.

Matthew 2:1 _____

Matthew 4:13 _____

Matthew 14:34 _____

Matthew 15:29 _____

Matthew 16:13 _____

Matthew 21:1 _____

# JESUS: "FOLLOW ME!"

CAROL ELLIS

After Jesus' baptism and His time of temptation in the wilderness, Jesus moved to Capernaum (kuh PUHR nay uhm), a fishing town by the Sea of Galilee. He began to preach, calling for people to repent (turn from) their sins.

One day, as Jesus walked along the shore of the Sea of Galilee, He noticed two men, Simon Peter and his brother, Andrew, throwing a net into the water. Simon Peter and Andrew were fishermen. They used nets to catch fish. Jesus called to the men, "Follow Me, and I will make you fish for people!"
◎ How do you think the men responded? How would you have responded?
◎ What do you think Jesus meant when he told Simon Peter and Andrew they would fish for people?

Read Matthew 4:18-20. According to verse 20, Simon Peter and Andrew immediately stopped fishing and accepted Jesus' invitation to follow Him! That means they didn't go pack a suitcase or say good-bye to their friends. Simon Peter and Andrew stopped what they were doing and followed Jesus.

Read Matthew 4:21-22. Imagine Jesus continuing His walk along the Sea of Galilee. He saw two more fishermen, James and John, in a boat with their father. Jesus also invited the brothers to follow Him. Did you notice in verse 22 what the men did?

Yes! They immediately left the boat—and their father—and followed Jesus!

Eventually Jesus called 12 men to be His first disciples (or apostles). You can find the names of the 12 disciples in Matthew 10:2-4. They are: Peter (Simon Peter), Andrew, James (the son of Zebedee), John, Philip, Bartholomew, Thomas, Matthew, James (the son of Alphaeus), Thaddaeus, Simon (the Zealot), and Judas Iscariot.

The disciples left everything—their jobs, families, and friends—to follow Jesus. They chose to put Jesus first above everything else in their lives.
◎ Why do you think the men chose to follow Jesus?
◎ Why did you choose to follow Jesus?

The disciples spent time with Jesus and learned from Him about living in ways that please God. They tried to do what Jesus said and to follow His example of serving other people. And do you remember what Jesus told Simon Peter and Andrew they would do if they followed Him? Jesus told them they would "fish for people." That means they would help people know about Jesus, the Savior. As the disciples followed Jesus, they told people about Him.

Since you've asked Jesus to be your Savior and Lord, you're a Christian—a follower of Jesus! Write in this space when you became a follower of Jesus:

_____

## DAY 1 — PUT GOD FIRST

VERSES OF THE DAY: Matthew 22:37-38
CHALLENGE: Matthew 16:24-25

**DO!** In the first column, list the 10 most important things or people in your life. In the second column, number the things or people from 1 (most important) to 10 (least important) in order of importance to you.

| IMPORTANT THINGS/PEOPLE | ORDER OF IMPORTANCE |
| --- | --- |
| | |
| | |
| | |
| | |
| | |
| | |
| | |
| | |
| | |
| | |

Look back at your list. Did you include God? If so, what number of importance did you give Him? If not, why not?

Read Matthew 22:37-38 again. God wants you to love Him with all your heart, soul, and mind! That means you will put God first in your life!

✓ God wants to be Lord (or boss) of your life.
✓ God wants you to give Him your best—the best of your time, talents, and things.
✓ God wants you to want what He wants, not what you want.

**PRAY** Thank God for inviting you to follow Jesus. Ask God to help you put Him first by letting Him be Lord of your life.

## DAY 2 — SPEND TIME WITH GOD

VERSE OF THE DAY: Matthew 6:33
CHALLENGE: 2 Timothy 3:16-17

**DO!** Think about your best friend. Write his or her name here: _____
Now, draw a picture of your best friend.

Answer the following questions:
? What are some ways you spend time with your best friend?

? How much time do you spend with your friend every day (or most days) in person or talking/chatting/texting?

? What are some ways you spend time with God?

? How much time do you spend with God every day (or most days)?

? What changes do you need to make in order to spend more time with God?

✓ God wants you to spend time with Him by praying and reading your Bible every day.
✓ God not only wants you to talk to Him, He wants you to listen to Him.

**PRAY** Ask God to help you make the changes you need to spend more time with Him.

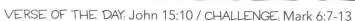

## DAY 3

# DO WHAT JESUS SAID

VERSE OF THE DAY: John 15:10 / CHALLENGE: Mark 6:7-13

**DO!** What do you think of when you hear the word *command*? Do you picture a person giving orders or instructions to someone to do something?

List three "commands" you are to obey at home or at school:

1.
2.
3.

Do you know any commands Jesus gave His followers? If so, write a few of them here:

Discover some of Jesus' commands by working the crossword puzzle on page 30.

**KNOW!**

✓ Jesus taught about faith, trust, and obedience to God.

✓ You can study the Bible to learn what Jesus said for His followers to do.

✓ Jesus wants you to not only learn what He said, He wants you to do what He said!

**PRAY** Thank God for the Bible that helps you learn about Jesus' commands. Ask God to help you do what Jesus said.

## DAY 4

# FOLLOW JESUS' EXAMPLE

VERSES OF THE DAY: John 13:14-15 / CHALLENGE: John 13:1-20

**DO!** Match these Bible verses to the examples of how Jesus related to God and other people:

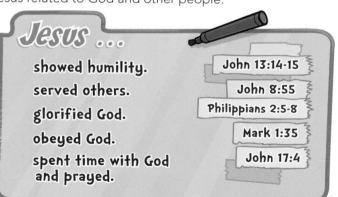

*Jesus ...*

showed humility.
served others.
glorified God.
obeyed God.
spent time with God and prayed.

John 13:14-15
John 8:55
Philippians 2:5-8
Mark 1:35
John 17:4

Put a check mark next to one of Jesus' actions you can do this week to be like Him.

**KNOW!**

✓ Jesus followed God's plan for His life by leaving heaven and coming to earth.

✓ Jesus is your example for the way to relate to God and how you treat other people.

✓ You can learn about Jesus' examples by reading the Bible.

**PRAY** Thank God for the examples Jesus gave you for how to live in ways that please Him. Ask God to help you follow Jesus' example this week.

## DAY 5 — TELL OTHERS ABOUT JESUS

VERSES OF THE DAY: Matthew 28:19-20
CHALLENGE: John 4:1-29,39-42

 **DO!** Do you remember what Jesus said to Simon Peter and Andrew when He first met them? (You can check out the story again in Matthew 4:18-22.)

Fill in the missing words:
Jesus said, "_____, and I will make you _____." That meant they would tell other people about Jesus.

In today's verses (Matthew 28:19-20), Jesus' life on earth was coming to an end. He commanded the disciples to "Go, and make _____."

What are some ways you can tell other people about Jesus?

**KNOW!**
✓ All Christians are commanded to tell other people about Jesus.
✓ You can tell people about Jesus by telling what He has done for you.
✓ The Holy Spirit will help you tell other people about Jesus.

 **PRAY** Ask God to help you tell someone about Jesus this week.

## DAY 6 — BE STRONG

VERSE OF THE DAY: Psalm 31:24
CHALLENGE: John 15:18-27

**DO!** Picture this: You are invited to spend Saturday night with a friend, but your parents won't let you because you have church in the morning. Your friend begins to make fun of you for going to church and believing in God. What would you say?

Your response: I would say ...

### BE STRONG! STAND UP FOR WHAT YOU BELIEVE!
→ Know what you believe and why you believe it.
→ Pray for the Holy Spirit to help you tell people what you believe.
→ Do not argue with people about what you believe.
→ Live out what you believe!

**KNOW!**
✓ Life will get hard sometimes because you follow Jesus.
✓ The Holy Spirit will help you be strong as you honor God with your life.
✓ You can live with joy regardless of your circumstances.

 **PRAY** Thank God for always being with you. Ask God to help you be strong and tell others what you believe, even when it is difficult.

# JESUS' COMMANDS

Check out some of Jesus' commands! Fill in the blanks by reading the Scripture verses, then use the missing words to complete the crossword puzzle.

**ACROSS:**

3. _____ to God (Matthew 11:15).

4. Love your _____ (Matthew 5:44).

9. _____ others (Matthew 18:21-22).

10. Seek first the _____ of God (Matthew 6:33).

11. Do not _____ (Matthew 7:1).

12. Do not _____ about your life (Matthew 6:25).

**DOWN**

1. _____ your parents (Matthew 15:4).

2. Make and baptize _____ (Matthew 28:19).

5. Love your _____ (Matthew 22:39).

6. Ask, _____ , knock (Matthew 7:7-8).

7. _____ the Lord (Matthew 22:37).

8. _____ Me (Matthew 4:19).

## WORD BANK

follow
listen
seek
forgive
disciples
honor
enemies
judge
love
kingdom
neighbor
worry

# JESUS' DISCIPLES

Unscramble the letters in the boxes below to discover the names of Jesus' disciples. Write the names in the spaces. If you need help, read the Bible verses or check out Matthew 10:2-4.

HNJO _____ was a fisherman on the Sea of Galilee with his father Zebedee and his brother, James. Jesus called him to be a disciple while he was repairing nets (Matthew 4:21-22). He helped Peter prepare the Passover meal (Luke 22:8). From the cross, Jesus told him to care for His mother (John 19:26-27).

The Bible tells nothing about MJSAE _____ except for his name.

DDAAETUSH _____ (or JDSUA _____) asked Jesus how He was going to reveal Himself to the disciples and not to the world (John 14:22).

WAEDRN _____ was a fisherman with his brother, Simon Peter, on the Sea of Galilee. Jesus called him to be a disciple while he was fishing (Matthew 4:18-20). He brought his brother, Simon Peter, to Jesus (John 1:40-42), and told Jesus about the boy with the loaves and fishes (John 6:8-9).

SJEAM _____ was a fisherman on the Sea of Galilee with his father Zebedee and his brother, John. Jesus called him to be a disciple while he was repairing nets (Matthew 4:21-22). He was the first disciple to be killed for his faith.

The Bible tells us nothing about OIMSN _____ except for his name.

WBEARMOTLOH _____ (or AAAELTNHN _____) was invited to see Jesus by Philip. Jesus called him a "true Israelite" (John 1:45-51).

SUJAD RTICSOAI _____ _____ was the keeper of the disciples' money bag. He betrayed Jesus for 30 pieces of silver (Matthew 26:15). He was sorry for what he had done and hanged himself (Matthew 27:3-5).

Jesus called TTAWEMH _____ to be a disciple while he was a tax collector in Capernaum. He invited his friends to a dinner where they could meet Jesus (Matthew 9:9-13).

NIOSM EERPT _____ _____ was a fisherman with his brother, Andrew, on the Sea of Galilee. Jesus called him to be a disciple while he was fishing (Matthew 4:18-20). Jesus helped him walk on water (Matthew 14:29). He denied Jesus before His crucifixion (Luke 22:54-62) and was later forgiven by Jesus (John 21:15-19).

AHMSOT _____ encouraged the disciples to go with Jesus and die with Him (John 11:16). He wanted proof that Jesus had risen from the dead (John 20:25). Jesus showed him His hands and side to prove His resurrection (John 20:27).

Jesus called HPIILP _____ to follow Him as a disciple (John 1:43). He found Nathanael and told him about Jesus (John 1:43-45). He went with Andrew to bring some Greeks to Jesus (John 12:20-22).

# JESUS: THE SERMON ON THE MOUNT

## KLISTA STORTS

Jesus traveled all over Galilee, preaching, teaching, and healing. Because of His work, people heard about Him and brought sick friends to be healed. Many people followed Him from city to city. On one occasion, when Jesus saw the crowds, He went up on a hillside and began teaching. Although Jesus was speaking to His disciples, the rest of the crowd listened too. The words Jesus spoke that day are found in Matthew 5–7. These verses are known as the Sermon on the Mount. During His sermon, Jesus used words to help the people know how to live in ways that pleased God.

Jesus used illustrations, such as being salt and light, to remind people when they become His followers, they are not to keep that good news to themselves. Think about salt. A small amount of salt added to food can make a big difference. But if salt sits on a shelf too long, or gets diluted by water, the salt loses its ability to make a difference. Now think about light. Even a small light in a dark room makes a big difference. If the light is hidden under a basket, though, the light doesn't do any good! Jesus said His followers are to be like salt and light—making a difference in the lives of other people by sharing the good news about Him.

Jesus also gave instructions about the relationships people have with one another. Jesus reminded His disciples the way to show others their love for Him was to love their enemies. Wait! Did you read that right? Love their enemies? Yes, that's right! Jesus said His followers should love and pray for people who treat them wrongly. That can be hard to do, but God helps His followers love other people— even those who are difficult to love.

During His sermon, Jesus told people not to worry about anything—not the clothes they wear or the food they eat—nothing. He knows the needs people have before they do! But although Jesus knows what people need, He still wants them to pray. Jesus even gave a model prayer in His sermon! The prayer helps people know they can ask Jesus for small things, like bread to eat, as well as big things, like forgiveness for sins.

This week, you will take a closer look at the Sermon on the Mount. As you work through your journal each day, you will discover you can use the same words Jesus spoke to the disciples many years ago to help you live a life that honors God today!

## DAY 1 — ATTITUDES TO BE

**VERSES OF THE DAY:** Matthew 5:3-11
**CHALLENGE:** Philippians 2:5-11

 **DO!** As Jesus began the "Sermon on the Mount," He started with what we call the Beatitudes. Write the letter of the "Attitude to Be" next to the "Beatitude" that matches it.

### BEATITUDE

___ 1. Poor in spirit
___ 2. Mourn
___ 3. Gentle or meek
___ 4. Hunger and thirst for righteousness
___ 5. Merciful
___ 6. Pure in heart
___ 7. Peacemaker
___ 8. Persecuted for righteousness

### ATTITUDE TO BE

A. Focus on being godly, not worldly
B. Consider others first above myself
C. Stand strong even when the world makes fun of my beliefs
D. Desire to be all God wants me to be
E. Aware of my sinfulness, not prideful
F. Offer forgiveness because I've been forgiven
G. Sad or sorry over sin
H. Don't argue, help friends "get along"

Choose one of the Beatitudes above and list specific ways you can show that attitude this week.

_____

**KNOW!**
✓ *Blessed* means "happy."
✓ Following the Beatitudes can help people see Jesus lives in you.

**PRAY** Ask God to help you have an attitude like Jesus even when life gets difficult.

## DAY 2 — PASS THE SALT AND TURN ON THE LIGHT!

**VERSES OF THE DAY:** Matthew 5:13-16
**CHALLENGE:** Philippians 2:12-15

**DO!** On the salt shaker, write words that you can say to be an encouragement and show God's love to someone.

On the light bulb, draw a picture of or describe a situation where you can show that you're a Christian by an act of kindness.

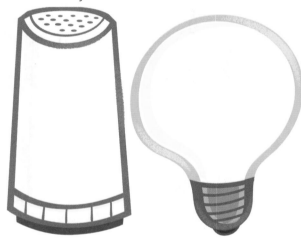

**KNOW!**
✓ Some people have never heard of Jesus. You may be the only one who can tell them about His love and forgiveness.
✓ The words you say and the things you do can help people want to know more about Jesus—or not.
✓ Studying your Bible and praying each day can help you be prepared to tell other people about Jesus.

**PRAY** Ask God to help your words be pleasing to Him and your actions reflect what He has done for you. Ask Him to help you have courage to tell others about Him.

Answers: 1-E; 2-G; 3-B; 4-A; 5-F; 6-D; 7-H; 8-C

# DAY 3

## I HAVE TO LOVE *HIM?*

VERSE OF THE DAY: Matthew 5:44 / CHALLENGE: Matthew 5:38-48

**DO!** While you may feel you don't have any enemies, do you know people who have hurt you in some way?

Below are drawings of a school, church, and a house in a neighborhood. Write the initials of people in each of those places who may have hurt you and you need to pray for.

**KNOW!**

✓ Jesus said to love and pray for those who persecute or treat us wrongly.
✓ Jesus forgave us, so we must forgive others.

**PRAY** Take time to thank God for His love and forgiveness. As you pray, ask Him to help you forgive those on your list just as He forgave you.

---

# DAY 4

## THE MODEL PRAYER

VERSES OF THE DAY: Matthew 6:9-13 / CHALLENGE: Matthew 6:5-8

**DO!** Learn the parts of the Model Prayer. Match the symbols in the chart with the symbols in the next column, then use markers or crayons to color the rows to match the symbol colors. You will use one color twice.

| | |
|---|---|
| 🎺 | • Our Father in heaven, Your name be honored as holy. |
| 👍 | • Your kingdom come. Your will be done on earth as it is in heaven. |
| 🍞 | • Give us this day our daily bread. |
| ✝ | • And forgive us our debts, as we also have forgiven our debtors. |
| 🛡 | • And do not bring us into temptation, but deliver us from the evil one. |
| 🎺 | • For Yours is the kingdom and the power and the glory forever. Amen. |

🛡 **Help and protection**
🍞 **Dependence**
🎺 **Praise**
👍 **Obedience**
✝ **forgiveness**

**KNOW!**

✓ God knows your needs, but still wants to hear from you.
✓ As you pray, you will become more aware of the ways God provides for and protects you.

**PRAY**  Using Jesus' example, draw a picture or write your own prayer to God.

# DAY 5

## NO WORRIES!

VERSE OF THE DAY: Matthew 6:25
CHALLENGE: Matthew 6:25-34

**DO!** Jesus said the flowers and birds don't worry about what to wear or eat, because God takes care of them. He loves you much more than flowers and birds, so you know He'll take care of you! Write on the petals of the flower or the feathers of the bird things you are worried about. As God takes care of each of those worries, color in the petals or feathers until the picture is complete.

**K.NOW!**

✓ God loves people more than anything else He created. He knows your needs.
✓ Sometimes His answer to your prayer may be: No. You may not always get what you want, but you will always have what you need.

**PRAY** Thank God for the way He provides for and takes care of you even before you know what you need. If you are worried about something, ask God for His help, then trust He will answer in the way that is best for you.

# DAY 6

## ROCK SOLID

VERSE OF THE DAY: Matthew 7:24
CHALLENGE: Matthew 7:24-27

**DO!** Jesus said we should live our lives based on the words He has spoken. In the word search, find some of the words He spoke: birds, blessed, flowers, forgive, gentle, happy, light, love, mercy, obedient, peace, praise, pray, pure, righteous, salt, trust.

```
W K E Q T J F P C P G L J V U
V K G X R N U U R R P V R I Y
P B L E S S E D L A L L K P V
A V G M S A S I V I Y J P I K
L S F G J N A D D S M A J R X
S U O E T H G I R E H H R T W
G T L A S H M F R I B E B S K
G E Y G M Y E C E X B O S U U
U P N A V V Y V N L X O R R O
Q Q S T I L I G H T P C E T O
V R B G L F E Q I L U F W X Q
Z L R A F E W H O E R W O Q X
S O E C A E P V G V E V L W D
F E U I D J E T Y E Y G F U N
J C M A I A P O P V K R V T B
```

✓ The words in the Bible can help you know how to live for Jesus.
✓ You can trust God to help and take care of you.

**PRAY** Thank God for the Bible and the important messages He shares through it. Ask Him to help you remember these words as you try to live in a way that honors Him.

# BOOKS OF THE BIBLE

Look at the names of the books of the Bible. Fill in the names of the missing Bible books, then number the divisions in the correct order, beginning with "The Law."

The 39 books of the Old Testament tell the story of God's chosen people, the Israelites. The books describe the promised Messiah, who is necessary to restore people's relationship with God. The New Testament's 27 books tell how Jesus—the Messiah—came to fulfill what was written in the Old Testament and give instructions about following Him!

## Old Testament

### The Law
Genesis, Exodus, Leviticus, Deuteronomy

### Poetry
Job, Psalms, Ecclesiastes, Song of Songs

### History
Joshua, Judges, 1 & 2 Samuel, 1 & 2 Kings, 1 & 2 Chronicles, Ezra, Esther

### Major Prophets
Isaiah, Jeremiah, Lamentations, Ezekiel

### Minor Prophets
Hosea, Joel, Amos, Obadiah, Micah, Nahum, Habakkuk, Zephaniah, Zechariah, Malachi

# New Testament

**History**
Acts

**Gospels**
Matthew
Luke
John

**Paul's Letters**
Romans
1 & 2 Corinthians
Galatians
Philippians
Colossians
1 & 2 Thessalonians
1 & 2 Timothy
Philemon

**Prophecy**
Revelation

**General Letters**
Hebrews
1 & 2 Peter
1, 2, & 3 John
Jude

# JESUS: THE PARABLES

TODD CAPPS

Do you enjoy listening to someone tell a good story? What makes the story come alive for you? Can you remember the story well enough to retell it? What did you learn from the story?

Imagine spending time with Jesus. One afternoon, a large crowd of people gathered to listen to Him. He began, "A farmer went out into his fields to sow some seeds." Jesus told how some of the seeds fell on rocky ground, some fell among thorns, some were eaten by birds, and some of the seeds actually took root and grew. Would you think, *Jesus is a great storyteller, He knows a lot about farming and how important it is for the seeds to be planted correctly?* While you may think this, Jesus had another reason for telling this story. He communicated an important lesson to the people listening to Him.

Jesus used stories to help people learn about God. The stories Jesus used are called *parables. Parables* are "stories using common, everyday items to illustrate what the storyteller wants to communicate." What message do you think Jesus wanted the people to understand about the seeds? Read Matthew 13:1-9 for the whole parable.

Parables create minidramas that tell what is taking place. They communicate a simple story related to the item being described as well as a deeper meaning, helping the listener understand something about God. For example, Jesus told the parable of the seed to illustrate that some people will reject God's messages (seeds on rocky ground), some will believe for a short time then allow others to change their understanding of God (grow among the thorns), some people will be led to believe untrue things (seeds eaten by the birds), and some people will believe and grow in what they know about God (seeds that take root).

In addition to telling parables, Jesus took time to explain what the parables meant. Many times Jesus waited until He was alone with the disciples to explain a parable. He did this to make sure the disciples understood what He was teaching. Jesus knew some of the people who heard His parables would not understand them because the people did not listen with the right attitude. These people refused to allow God to speak to them through the parables. They had already decided they did not want to know what Jesus taught.

As you read and study some of Jesus' parables, ask God to help you understand the meaning behind them and to learn something new about God. Look for the main points of the parables.

This week we will explore six of the parables Jesus told.

## DAY 1 — THE GOOD SAMARITAN

VERSES OF THE DAY: Luke 10:25-37 / CHALLENGE: Deuteronomy 6:5; Leviticus 19:18

**DO!** Write the name of the person(s) from the Bible story (Luke 10:25-37) each statement describes.

Asked how he could have eternal life.

Asked what the law said.

Asked, "Who is my neighbor?"

Told a parable.

Robbed and left on the side of the road.

Refused to help the hurt man.

Helped the hurt man.

Said, "Go and do the same thing."

**KNOW!**

✓ God wants you to love Him with every part of yourself (heart, soul, mind, body).

✓ God wants you to love and care for all people.

✓ God created each person unique and in His image.

✓ God cares for each person.

**PRAY** Ask God to help you be like the Samaritan and care for all people regardless of skin color, nationality, language, or anything else.

## DAY 2 — THE LOST SON

VERSES OF THE DAY: Luke 15:11-32 / CHALLENGE: Matthew 18:10-14

**DO!** Follow the son's path. Read the Bible verses as you move along the path.

Start

Luke 15:11-13

Luke 15:14

Luke 15:20-21

Luke 15:15-16

Luke 15:17-19

Luke 15:22-24

Luke 15:25-30

Luke 15:31-32

End

**KNOW!**

✓ The Father represents God.

✓ The younger son represents you.

✓ You make many decisions that do not please God.

✓ God is always waiting for you to choose obedience and come back to Him.

✓ God knows what is best for you.

**PRAY** Ask God to help you obey Him every day. Ask Him to forgive you when you do not listen and do things your own way. Thank God that He forgives you when you disobey Him.

## THE LOST SHEEP

VERSES OF THE DAY: Matthew 18:12-14
CHALLENGE: John 10:7-18

**DO!** Count the sheep on the page. How many can you find? ___

How would you feel if you owned 100 sheep, but could only find 99? Would you be concerned about the one lost sheep? Would you leave the 99 to go find the one?

**KNOW!**
- ✓ Many times the Bible refers to people as sheep.
- ✓ Sheep recognize the voice of their shepherd.
- ✓ Jesus referred to Himself as "The Good Shepherd" (John 10:7-18).
- ✓ Jesus said a good shepherd would die for his sheep (John 10:11).
- ✓ Jesus is concerned for all of His sheep (us). He wants everyone to follow Him.

**PRAY** Thank God for Jesus, the Good Shepherd. Ask Him to help you learn His voice and follow everything He says.

## THE TALENTS

VERSES OF THE DAY: Matthew 25:14-30
CHALLENGE: Luke 19:12-27

**DO!** Read Matthew 25:14-30. Do the math:

| Given | | Earned | | Extra | = | Total |
|---|---|---|---|---|---|---|
| 5 | + | 5 | + | 1 | = | |
| 2 | + | 2 | + | 0 | = | |
| 1 | + | 0 | – | 1 | = | |

How did the master respond to each person?

List the talents and abilities God has given you.

How can you use them to serve God?

**KNOW!**
- ✓ The Bible uses the word *talents* to mean money.
- ✓ We use the word to mean special skills we have, such as singing, drawing, acting, dancing, and so forth.
- ✓ God has given you talents and abilities to serve Him.
- ✓ Using your talents and abilities is a great way to tell people about God.

**PRAY** Thank God for the talents and abilities He has given you. Ask Him to help you use them to serve Him.

## DAY 5

# THE FOUNDATIONS

VERSES OF THE DAY: Luke 6:46-49 / CHALLENGE: 1 Corinthians 3:10-15

**DO!** Complete the dot-to-dots.

**Solid Foundation**

**Weak Foundation**

Based on Luke 6:46-49, how would you describe a person with a strong foundation? With a weak foundation?

**KNOW!**

✓ A foundation provides support and strength.

✓ A spiritual foundation is made of things you believe to be true.

✓ You build a spiritual foundation when you read the Bible, pray, worship, and listen to and obey God.

**PRAY** Ask God to help you develop a strong spiritual foundation so you can stand up for what you believe.

## DAY 6

# THE PHARISEE AND THE TAX COLLECTOR

VERSES OF THE DAY: Luke 18:9-14 / CHALLENGE: Luke 11:1-4

**DO!** Compare the two men praying. Draw a line from each statement to the person it describes.

Humble

Proud

God forgive me

I give a tenth of everything

I want people to see and hear me

I fast two times a week

Thank You I am not like other people

**KNOW!**

✓ God notices when and how you pray.

✓ God does not want you to compare yourself to other people.

✓ God wants you to examine your life and confess the things you have done.

✓ God wants you to ask for forgiveness.

✓ God does not want you to think you are better than other people.

**PRAY** Ask God to give you the right attitude about prayer.

# TEST YOUR BIBLE KNOWLEDGE

Read each question. Use the Word Bank to help you decide the answer. Still need help? Find the answers in your Bible. Write the answers in the puzzle.

## ACROSS

1. Who buried Isaac? (Genesis 35:29)

2. Who's wife told him to curse God and die? (Job 2:9)

4. What Roman military leader did Peter baptize? (Acts 10:23-48)

6. Who built the first temple in Jerusalem? (1 Kings 6)

8. What New Testament prophet said a famine would impact the whole world? (Acts 11:28)

9. Who was David's first wife? (1 Samuel 18:27)

12. Who was the commander of Solomon's army? (1 Kings 4:4)

16. What husband and wife died after lying about the amount of money they received for selling some land? (Acts 5:1-10)

18. Who fasted for 40 days on Mount Sinai? (Exodus 34:27-28)

## DOWN

1. Who was told to cut off his hair and throw one third of it in the wind? (Ezekiel 1:3; 5:2)

2. Whose daughter did Jesus raise from the dead? (Luke 8:41-42,49-55)

3. What man was famous for eating locusts? (Matthew 3:4)

5. Who is the most talked about woman in the Bible?

7. Who became a leper after he lied to Elisha? (2 Kings 5:27)

10. What king fasted after Daniel was thrown into the lions' den? (Daniel 6:6,18)

11. Who planted the first garden? (Genesis 2:8)

13. Who is the second woman named in the Bible? (Genesis 4:19)

14. Methuselah lived to be 969 years old. The second oldest man was 962 years old. Who was he? (Genesis 5:20)

15. Who was a teacher of Paul's? (Acts 22:3)

17. Who was the first man stoned to death because he believed in Jesus? (Acts 7:59)

## Word Bank

Adah
Agabus
Ananias and Sapphira
Benaiah
Cornelius
Darius
Esau and Jacob
Ezekiel
Gamaliel
Gehazi
God
Jared
Jairus
Job
John the Baptist
Michal
Moses
Sarah
Solomon
Stephen

# JESUS: THE MIRACLES

TRACEY ROGERS

"That was a miracle!" "Only a miracle will help us now." Have you heard comments like this at sporting events, when someone who was ill recovered, or when someone got a job after being unemployed for a long time?

What are *miracles*? *Miracles* are "unusual events that only God can cause to happen." Only God can perform miracles! Sometimes miracles are called *signs* and *wonders* because we just cannot explain what happens.

Read Matthew 4:23-24. Many of Jesus' miracles involved healing people. Jesus healed people who had diseases and sicknesses. People saw and heard about Jesus' healing power, so they brought many other people who had a variety of problems to Him to be healed. What types of people were brought to Jesus (v. 24)?

Why did Jesus perform miracles? Some reasons include:
1. To show people He is God's Son.
2. To prove His teaching and preaching.
3. To show He loved people.
4. To meet the physical needs of people.

Jesus knew people's physical needs must be met before their spiritual needs could be met. What are some physical needs?

_____

_____

Water, food, clothes, and shelter are the basic physical needs. Our physical well-being is a need too. Jesus healed those with sickness, disease, affliction, and demon possession. Why meet these needs first? We tend to focus on our problems, illnesses, diseases, and so forth first before thinking of our spiritual needs. When our physical needs are taken care of, we are open to hear the gospel of Jesus Christ. Do you focus on problems instead of Jesus?

Many of the people who personally experienced a miracle praised Jesus and told of the miracles, but some did not (see Luke 17:11-19). Would you praise Jesus if a miracle happened to you? Do you know someone who has experienced a miracle? Is he thankful to God for the miracle?

Over the next few days, we'll look at different types of miracles Jesus performed. Jesus not only healed people, He fed them, and raised some from the dead. Jesus also helped people catch fish, calmed storms, and even caused someone to walk on water! Imagine yourself in each story. How would you react each time? With belief? Doubt? Amazement?

## DAY 1 — HEALING

VERSE OF THE DAY: Matthew 17:18
CHALLENGE: Matthew 17:14-21

**DO!** Read Matthew 17:18. After the disciples failed to heal this boy, his father took him to Jesus. Jesus healed the boy, then explained that healing takes faith.

Read each Scripture passage and write the number of the healing that matches the verses.

1. Stooped woman        _____ Matthew 9:32-33

2. Lame man             _____ Mark 7:24-30

3. Demon-possessed man  _____ Luke 6:6-11

4. Withered hand        _____ John 5:5-9

5. Woman's daughter     _____ Luke 13:10-13

**KNOW!**

✓ You can ask God to help people.
✓ Sometimes the ways God chooses to heal or perform miracles are not the ways we might want.
✓ You can trust that God's plan is best.
✓ Faith comes through prayer and fasting (to go without food or drink for a time).

**PRAY** Ask God to heal people at your church, in your family, and your neighborhood.

## DAY 2 — FEEDING

VERSE OF THE DAY: John 6:11
CHALLENGE: John 6:1-14

**DO!** Five thousand men, plus women and children, had gathered to see Jesus! They were hungry, so Jesus decided to feed them. Color the dots to reveal what the people were fed.

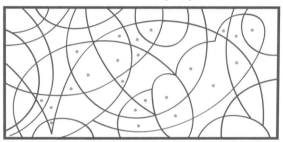

Jesus fed the people fish and bread. Read John 6:9.

? How many fish did Jesus have? _____
? How many loaves of bread did Jesus have? _____

? Read John 6:13. How much food was left over? _____

**KNOW!**

✓ Jesus meets the physical needs of people. You can help meet the hunger needs of people by giving food or money donations to church ministries or local rescue missions.
✓ Jesus thanked God for the food and trusted Him to provide. Each time you eat, you can thank God for the food He provides.
✓ God provided more food than was needed. You can be thankful when God blesses you with more than you need.
✓ Jesus' miracles helped people know He was the promised prophet. You can realize who Jesus is and that He still performs miracles.

**PRAY** Thank God for feeding you physically and spiritually.

# DAY 3

## FISHING

VERSES OF THE DAY: Luke 5:5-6 / CHALLENGE: Luke 5:1-11

 See how fast you can work this maze.

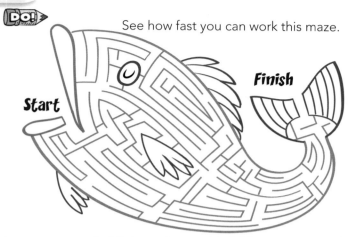

**Start**

**Finish**

Jesus commanded Peter to let out his fishing nets to catch some fish. Although Peter had not caught any fish all night, he obeyed Jesus and threw the nets out again. Read Luke 5:6. How would you explain what happened?

✓ In early Christian churches, the Greek word for *fish* (ichthus) came to be a symbol for Jesus. Later, the fish became a Christian symbol.

✓ Jesus told the disciples to follow Him and He would make them "fishers of men."

✓ You can be a "fisher of men" today by telling people about Jesus.

**PRAY** Pray for opportunities to "fish" for Jesus by telling people about Him.

# DAY 4

## WALKING

VERSES OF THE DAY: Matthew 14:25,29 / CHALLENGE: Matthew 14:22-33

**DO!** Fill a bowl or pan with water and place these items into the water: coin, spoon, leaf, rock, bar of soap, crayon, straw. Which items floated? Which items sank?

Have you ever tried to walk on water? Read Matthew 14:25,29 and write the names of the people who walked on water:

Find the following words in the puzzle: Peter, Jesus, walk, water, boat, disciples, afraid, sink.

```
B T X C I L S H D X
M O S R N P U I N Y
D I A R F A S U R Z
N D P T E C E P Y L
A H A Z I T J P R H
Y N H P U B E E U A
B H L J P S T P S M
K E U L M A Y V I T
S S I X W Y V Y N G
Q W A L K Z E A K F
```

✓ Jesus walked on water, and He caused Peter to walk on water too.

✓ The miracle of walking on water led those on the boat to worship Jesus. They knew Jesus is the Son of God.

**PRAY** Thank Jesus for doing things no one else can do. Thank Him for loving people enough to perform miracles.

## DAY 5 — RAISING

VERSES OF THE DAY: John 11:43-44
CHALLENGE: John 11:1-7,14-15,38-44

 Write the names of the items. Cross out the letters that are subtracted. Write the remaining letters in the spaces to solve the puzzle.

Jesus raised ___ ___ ___ ___ ___ ___ ___ from the dead.

Jesus raised people from the dead—young and old. Jesus was a close friend of Lazarus. The Scripture says Jesus loved Lazarus, so why did Jesus wait until Lazarus died to help him? Read John 11:41-42.

**KNOW**

✓ Jesus performed miracles so people who saw or experienced them would know He was sent from God to save people.
✓ Jesus had the power to bring Lazarus back to life.

**PRAY** Thank Jesus for saving you. Give praises for knowing you will some day live with Him forever in heaven.

## DAY 6 — CALMING

VERSE OF THE DAY: Luke 8:24
CHALLENGE: Luke 8:22-25

 Use the picture of the boat to help you draw the same boat in the empty grid.

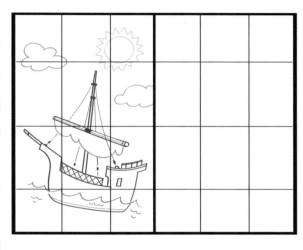

The weather on the Sea of Galilee is unpredictable. The weather changes all the time. Life can be like that as well. Unexpected things happen or your plans change. How do you feel when things don't go the way you plan?

**KNOW**

✓ The disciples went to Jesus for help, and Jesus calmed the sea.
✓ Jesus is ready to calm your fears and anger.
✓ You can have courage by trusting in God when you are afraid.
✓ Jesus has power over nature.

**PRAY** Thank God for the storms (difficult times) in your life, because you can learn and grow stronger in your walk with Him.

# MIRACLE STORIES IN THE GOSPELS

The first four books of the New Testament—Matthew, Mark, Luke, and John—are called the "Four Gospels." The Gospels tell about the life of Jesus. You can read about many of the miracles Jesus performed in more than one of the Gospels.

## 5,000 PEOPLE FED
- Matthew 14:15-21
- Mark 6:35-44
- Luke 9:12-17
- John 6:5-14

## DEMONS SENT INTO PIGS
- Matthew 8:28-34
- Mark 5:1-20
- Luke 8:26-39

## STORM CALMED
- Matthew 8:23-27
- Mark 4:35-41
- Luke 8:22-25

## JAIRUS' DAUGHTER RAISED
- Matthew 9:18-19,23-26
- Mark 5:22-24,35-43
- Luke 8:41-42,49-56

## SICK WOMAN HEALED
- Matthew 9:20-22
- Mark 5:25-34
- Luke 8:43-48

## PARALYTIC MAN HEALED
- Matthew 9:1-8
- Mark 2:1-12
- Luke 5:17-26

## LEPER HEALED
- Matthew 8:1-4
- Mark 1:40-45
- Luke 5:12-15

### PETER'S MOTHER-IN-LAW HEALED

- Matthew 8:14-15
- Mark 1:29-31
- Luke 4:38-39

### SHRIVELED HAND RESTORED

- Matthew 12:9-13
- Mark 3:1-5
- Luke 6:6-10

### BOY WITH EVIL SPIRIT HEALED

- Matthew 17:14-18
- Mark 9:14-27
- Luke 9:37-42

### JESUS WALKED ON WATER

- Matthew 14:22-33
- Mark 6:45-52
- John 6:16-21

### GIRL FREED FROM DEMON

- Matthew 15:21-28
- Mark 7:24-30

### BLIND MEN RECEIVE SIGHT

- Matthew 20:29-34
- Mark 10:46-52
- Luke 18:35-43

### FIG TREE CURSED

- Matthew 21:18-22
- Mark 11:12-14,20-24

### CENTURION'S SERVANT HEALED

- Matthew 8:5-13
- Luke 7:1-10

# JESUS: THE HEALINGS

TIM POLLARD

Have you ever been sick? Have you ever stayed in the hospital? Do you know anyone who has either been sick or stayed in the hospital? What kinds of things do you do when you are sick?

Even though you became a Christian, you will still get sick. People get sick because of sin in the world. God sent Jesus to earth to forgive people of their sin problem, but that doesn't mean that sickness isn't still a part of their lives. In Bible times there were many people who were sick. The good news is that Jesus traveled to many places and made people well! Read Matthew 9:35. Many other verses in the New Testament also tell about Jesus healing people.

Why is it important for Christians to know Jesus is our healer? You might wonder why some people are healed from diseases and other people are not. Maybe God didn't heal a family member the way you thought He should have. Take comfort that God knows what is happening in your life and He will help you even in loss.

Over the next few days we're going to take a look at six of Jesus' healing miracles. If

Jesus healed people on earth, and Jesus now lives in heaven with God, does that mean healings have stopped? Not at all! God is still in the business of healing, but just not by a physical touch from Jesus' hand. Here are a few things you can remember about healing:

- Sickness results from sin. Because of Adam and Eve's original sin, their punishment was death (they would one day die—Genesis 3:19). The penalty of death also brought with it disease and sickness. God did not create sickness, but it does exist because of sin.
- God does not use sickness as punishment for sin. God does not punish your personal sin by making you sick. People do get sick because of their sin, but it is not a punishment *for* sin. When you became a Christian, Jesus' death on the cross paid for your sin. Jesus has already been punished for your sin.
- God heals. God may use doctors and nurses to help bring about healing, but all healing ultimately comes from God.
- In heaven, there is no sickness, pain, or death (Revelation 21:4)!

## PETER'S MOTHER-IN-LAW

VERSES OF THE DAY: Matthew 8:14-15 / CHALLENGE: Mark 1:29-31

**DO!** Peter's mother-in-law was sick with a fever. (Peter was one of the disciples.) Jesus touched the woman's hand and she was made well.

Think about the last time you were sick with a fever. Draw or make a list of the things you would do if you were home from school because you were sick.

Did you remember to pray the last time you were sick?

 **KNOW!**

✓ God cares about things like fevers and wants to heal people who are sick.

✓ God wants you to pray for healing when you or other people are sick.

**PRAY** Thank God that He cares about things like fevers and sore throats. Ask God to help you remember to pray when you are well and when you are sick.

## A BLIND MAN

VERSES OF THE DAY: John 9:1-12 / CHALLENGE: John 9:13-34

**DO!** Place a pencil at the starting point, close your eyes, and work the maze. When you think you've reached the finish point, open your eyes. How did you do?

→ Now, keep your eyes open and draw a path through the maze. Was it easier or more difficult to complete the task with your eyes open?

→ Imagine how the blind man must have felt when he could finally see!

 **KNOW!**

✓ Jesus said the man was not blind because of his sin or the sins of his parents.

✓ Jesus spread mud on the man's eyes and told him to wash in a nearby pool.

✓ The healed man told other people what Jesus had done for him.

✓ You can tell other people about the things Jesus does for you.

**PRAY** Thank God for healing sick people. Ask God to help people who have trouble seeing or who can't see at all.

# DAY 3
## A MAN WHO COULD NOT SPEAK

VERSES OF THE DAY: Mark 7:31-37
CHALLENGE: Matthew 9:32-33

**DO!** Jesus healed a man who couldn't speak. Discover a word for someone who cannot speak by figuring out the code. On the blank, place either the letter before or the letter after the one given.

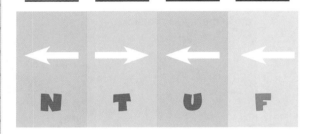

What is the longest time you have ever gone without talking? How would your life be different if you were not able to talk?

Sometimes people won't talk because they are afraid. What can you do to be friends with people who might be afraid to speak up?

**KNOW!**

✓ After Jesus put His fingers in the man's ears and spit, Jesus touched the man's tongue. The man was able to hear and speak.
✓ Jesus can heal people today.

**PRAY** Thank God that He still heals people. Ask God how you can get involved in helping people who cannot hear or speak.

# DAY 4
## A MAN WHO COULD NOT WALK

VERSES OF THE DAY: Mark 2:1-12
CHALLENGE: Mark 2:15-17

**DO!** These verses don't tell how the man felt when he was able to get up and walk. How do you think the man felt?

→ Draw a picture in Box #1 of yourself playing your favorite sport.
→ Think about this: How would not being able to use your legs affect your ability to participate in your favorite sport?
→ Draw a picture of yourself in Box #2 playing your favorite sport without using your legs.

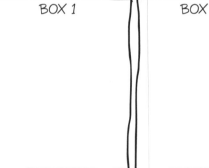

**KNOW!**

✓ Jesus forgave the man of his sin (spiritual healing) before He made the man able to walk (physical healing). Healing sin is what God cares about most.
✓ Just because sin is forgiven does not mean that a person will be healed physically.

**PRAY** Ask God to reveal the sin in your life. Ask God to forgive you for the sin you've committed. Thank Him for forgiving your sins.

## DAY 5

# TEN MEN WITH A SKIN DISEASE

VERSES OF THE DAY: Luke 17:11-19 / CHALLENGE: Mark 1:40-45

**DO!** Find the following items around your house. Touch the items and describe how they feel. Are they soft, hard, scratchy, or smooth?

**BASKET** — How it feels

**COUNTERTOP** — How it feels

**RUG** — How it feels

**CHAIR** — How it feels

→ Which texture did you like best?
→ Now touch your skin. Which texture that you felt is closest to your skin's texture?
→ How do you think the men felt when their skin disease was gone (Luke 17:11-19)?

 **KNOW!**

✓ Jesus was on His way to Jerusalem when He was met by 10 men who had a bad skin disease.
✓ Jesus healed all 10 men as they were going to the priests.
✓ One man returned and thanked Jesus, but the other nine went on their way.
✓ God wants us to be thankful for all situations in our lives.

**PRAY** Thank God for what He has done for you. Pray for people you know who have physical and spiritual needs.

---

## DAY 6

# JAIRUS' DAUGHTER

VERSES OF THE DAY: Luke 8:40-42,49-56 / CHALLENGE: John 11:1-43

**DO!** Find these words in the puzzle: heal, Jairus, Jesus, saves, sin.

What does each word have to do with the story you read in Luke 8?

Heal: _____

Jairus: _____

Jesus: _____

Saves: _____

Sin: _____

```
D J F N P M L Q
Y E I W I J A N
S S K P A N E P
O F U I R F H N
X Y R S E V A S
R U R A E K M D
S H R L X J E P
D X E U G P J A
```

 **KNOW!**

✓ The daughter of a church leader, Jairus, was very sick. Jairus asked Jesus to heal his daughter.
✓ Soon Jesus and Jairus were told that Jairus' daughter had died.
✓ Jesus went to the house and raised the girl back to life.
✓ Jesus saves people from sin and heals people.
✓ Jesus has the power to raise people from the dead.

**PRAY** Thank God that He is the one who saves from sin and brings healing to people.

# I CAN PRAY

When you pray, you talk to and listen to God. You can talk to God anywhere and at any time. You don't have to use special words or even close your eyes! You can talk to Him out loud or pray quietly to yourself. God wants you to talk to Him often!

The word  can help you remember things to share with God:

**P** stands for praise.

Praise God for who He is and for all He has done for you.

**R** stands for repent.

When you repent, you tell God what you've done wrong and turn or change from disobeying God to obeying Him.

**A** stands for ask.

God wants you to ask Him for the things other people need.

**Y** stands for yourself.

**God wants you to  for yourself too!**

Look at the "I Can Pray" hand. Now look at your hand and try to remember what each part of your hand represents. (With your parents' permission, you may want to write the *PRAY* letters on your fingers to help you remember!)

On the next page, make a prayer list by writing things to include in your prayers using the  letters.

### ⭐ CHALLENGE:
Memorize the Model Prayer Jesus taught His disciples (Matthew 6:9-13)!

**PARENT PAGE ALERT!**
This is another page you can share with your parents. After you memorize what the PRAY letters stand for, use your hand to explain to your parents about prayer. Encourage your parents to make a list of things to include in their prayers, then pray with your parents using your lists as a guide.

# PRAYER LIST

**P = PRAISE**

I can praise God for:

**R = REPENT**

I need to ask God to forgive me for:

**A = ASK**

I can ask God for these things other people need:

**Y = YOURSELF**

I can ask God for these things I need:

# JESUS: CHANGED LIVES

TODD CAPPS

If you wrote down the names of all the people you have ever met, how many would you list? How many of these people have made a real difference in your life? What was it about these people who changed your life?

During His time on earth, Jesus met a lot of people. The Bible does not tell us exactly how many, but it says crowds of people came to listen to Him teach. We know He fed over 5,000 people with one little boy's lunch (John 6:1-15). Do you think these people's lives were changed because of this event?

As Jesus traveled from city to city teaching about God, people were drawn to Him. Many people wanted Him to touch and heal them. Some people came for selfish reasons—they wanted to be healed, have Jesus touch their children, or wanted something else from Jesus. Some were drawn by what Jesus taught about God.

This week you will learn how Jesus changed the lives of some people, such as Simeon, Anna, Peter, Paul, Zacchaeus, and others. In the "Challenge" verses, you will discover even more people who were changed because they spent time with Jesus. As you read about these individuals, look for the reasons they followed Jesus. What did Jesus do for the people? How were their lives changed by Jesus?

Think about your life. How has Jesus changed your life? Write down some answers to these questions.

- What was my life like before I became a Christian?
- How did I learn about becoming a Christian?
- When did I ask Jesus to be my Savior and Lord?
- How has my life been different since becoming a Christian?
- How am I living in ways that please and honor God?
- Who am I telling about my relationship with Jesus?

Jesus is still changing people's lives today. When a person asks Jesus to be her Savior and Lord, Jesus changes her life. When a person commits to following God's plans for his life, Jesus is changing his life. When a person decides to honor God through his actions, attitudes, and words, Jesus is changing his life. In what ways does Jesus need to change your life?

## DAY 1 — SIMEON AND ANNA

VERSES OF THE DAY: Luke 2:21-40
CHALLENGE: Matthew 2:1-12

 Find a picture of yourself as a baby.

**PARENT PAGE ALERT!**

Ask your parents to answer these questions.

Who was the first person to hold me after I was born?

How old was I when I went to church the first time?

What did people say about me as a baby?

**KNOW!**

- ✓ Simeon dedicated his life to following God.
- ✓ God had promised Simeon he would not die until he saw the Messiah, Jesus.
- ✓ Simeon told Mary and Joseph about God's plans for Jesus.
- ✓ Anna lived at the temple, praising and worshiping God.
- ✓ Anna was 84 years old when she saw Baby Jesus.
- ✓ No one is too young or too old for God to change his life.

**PRAY** Thank God for sending Jesus. Ask God to help you know how He is working today.

## DAY 2 — NICODEMUS

VERSES OF THE DAY: John 3:1-21
CHALLENGE: John 7:50-51; 19:38-42

 If you could spend 30 minutes visiting with Jesus, what would you ask Him?

How would He respond to your questions?

**KNOW!**

- ✓ Even though Nicodemus was a member of the religious leaders, he did not understand who Jesus is or how a person could have a relationship with Jesus.
- ✓ Nicodemus went to Jesus at night so the other religious leaders would not know about the visit.
- ✓ John 3:16 presents the whole gospel in one verse.
- ✓ The term *rabbi* means "teacher."
- ✓ Nicodemus recognized Jesus as someone sent by God.
- ✓ Nicodemus helped bury Jesus' body (John 19:38-42).

**PRAY** Thank God that He loves all people and wants a relationship with them. Ask God to help you make a difference in the lives of people by telling them how they can have a relationship with Jesus.

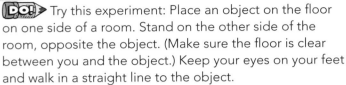

## DAY 3 — PETER

VERSES OF THE DAY: Matthew 4:18-22; 14:22-33 / CHALLENGE: Acts 10:1-48

**DO!** Try this experiment: Place an object on the floor on one side of a room. Stand on the other side of the room, opposite the object. (Make sure the floor is clear between you and the object.) Keep your eyes on your feet and walk in a straight line to the object.

❓ How did you do? How straight was the line you walked?

Return to your starting point and walk to the object again, but this time keep your eyes on the object as you walk.

❓ How did you do this time? Walking in a straight line is much easier when you keep your eyes on the object, isn't it?

✓ Peter was a fisherman with his brother Andrew.
✓ Peter was married and lived in Capernaum (Mark 1:21-31).

✓ Peter asked questions none of the other disciples would ask Jesus.
✓ *Faith* is "belief or trust."
✓ When Peter kept his eyes on Jesus, he had a lot of faith.
✓ Jesus told Peter he would be the beginning of the church.
✓ Herod planned to kill Peter.
✓ The church people prayed for Peter and God released him from jail.

**PRAY** Ask God to give you the type of faith Peter had—faith to walk on water, faith to do things no one else could do, faith to be willing to die for what you believe.

## DAY 4 — ZACCHAEUS

VERSES OF THE DAY: Luke 19:1-10 / CHALLENGE: Mark 2:13-17

**DO!** Draw a picture of each of your family members. Measure how tall each person is and write the height under the drawing.

❓ Who is the tallest in your family? _____
❓ Who is the shortest in your family? _____

✓ Zacchaeus was a chief tax collector. He collected extra money from people and kept it for himself.
✓ The name *Zacchaeus* in Hebrew means "innocent."

✓ Zacchaeus was short. He could not see over the other people.
✓ A sycamore tree is a combination of a "fig" tree and a "mulberry" tree.
✓ People were not happy about Jesus going to Zacchaeus' house.
✓ Zacchaeus repaid the people he had cheated.
✓ Jesus said He came to seek and save people who did not have a relationship with God.
✓ No one is too tall or too short for God to change her life.

**PRAY** Thank God for your physical health. Ask Him to help you live in ways that honor Him.

# DAY 5

## WOMAN AT THE WELL

VERSES OF THE DAY: John 4:1-26,39-42
CHALLENGE: John 13:1-17

**DO!** Connect the dots.

### KNOW!

✓ Jesus was a Jew.
✓ The woman was a Samaritan.
✓ Jews and Samaritans did not like one another.
✓ Women typically went to the well early in the morning before the temperature became hot.
✓ This woman went to the well around noon.
✓ Jesus spoke to the woman, breaking another custom—men did not speak to women in public.
✓ Jesus told the woman things no one knew about her.
✓ The woman recognized Jesus as the Messiah and told people in her town about Him.

**PRAY** Think about all the things God knows about you. Spend time talking with God, asking Him to change your life like He changed the woman's life.

# DAY 6

## PAUL

VERSES OF THE DAY: Acts 9:1-19
CHALLENGE: Acts 16:16-40

**DO!** Unscramble the letters to discover the books Paul wrote. Next to each book, write the page number the book begins on in your Bible.

TTSUI _____ (page __ )

ALSSSNHT1ENAIO _____ (page __ )

SANSAN2EHSTOLI _____ (page __ )

GSANLAATI _____ (page __ )

LENPIOMH _____ (page __ )

ONOICLSSAS _____ (page __ )

2SNAROCIHTIN _____ (page __ )

PPHNILIPSAI _____ (page __ )

THYMOIT1 _____ (page __ )

SENPHESAI _____ (page __ )

NTHCOR1IASNI _____ (page __ )

TOY2HMIT _____ (page __ )

ORSNMA _____ (page __ )

### KNOW!

→ Saul was present at the stoning of Stephen (Acts 7:57-58).
→ Saul was going to Damascus to arrest followers of Jesus.
→ A great light from heaven blinded Saul.
→ Saul is the same man as Paul.
→ Paul began teaching people about Jesus.
→ Paul wrote 13 books of the New Testament.
→ Paul was one of the first missionaries.
→ Paul was arrested for teaching people about Jesus.

**PRAY** Ask God to give you the courage to be like Paul, telling people everywhere you go about Jesus.

# ABCs OF BECOMING A CHRISTIAN

Becoming a Christian is the most important decision anyone can ever make.
Use the information on this page to tell people about Jesus.

## WHAT DOES THE BIBLE SAY ABOUT BECOMING A CHRISTIAN?

✓ God loves you (John 3:16).
✓ Sin is choosing your way instead of God's way. Sin separates people from God (Romans 3:23).
✓ God sent Jesus so you would not have to die for your sin. Jesus died on the cross, He was buried, and God raised Him from the dead (Romans 5:8).

## HOW TO BECOME A CHRISTIAN

### A

**ADMIT** to God you are a sinner (Romans 3:23). Repent, turn away from your sin (Acts 3:19; 1 John 1:9).

### B

**BELIEVE** that Jesus is God's Son and accept God's gift of forgiveness from sin (Acts 16:31; Acts 4:12; John 14:6; Ephesians 2:8-9).

### C

**CONFESS** your faith in Jesus Christ as Savior and Lord (Romans 10:9-10,13).

The Holy Spirit will help a person know when it is time to become a Christian.
If it is not time for your friend to become a Christian,
do not push her to do so. God will help her know the right time. If your friend
wants to become a Christian, you can help her pray a prayer like this:

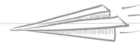

**DEAR GOD,**

I know I have sinned and my sin separates me from You. I am sorry for my sin. I believe Jesus died on the cross for me so my sin can be forgiven. I believe Jesus rose from the dead and is alive. God, please forgive me. I ask Jesus to come into my life and be my Savior and Lord. I will obey You and live for You the rest of my life. Thank You. In Jesus' name I pray, Amen.

# MY TESTIMONY

## MY STORY

A testimony is a story. When you share your testimony with someone, you are telling him about yourself. Each Christian should be able to tell how she became a Christian. Use these questions to help you write your testimony. Share your testimony with your friends this week.

I first started thinking about becoming a Christian when ...

To become a Christian, I needed to ...

When I became a Christian, I ...

My life is different since I became a Christian in these ways ...

I can help someone become a Christian by ...

# JESUS: HIS NAMES

TRACEY ROGERS

What does your name mean? _____ Why did your parents choose your name? _____

We are given a name at birth, but we may pick up nicknames as we grow. Sometimes we are called by names that speak about us—smart, tall, short, fast, kicker, good with math, soccer champ, and so on. Do you have a nickname? Who gave you the name?

The name *Jesus* is from the Hebrew word "Joshua," meaning "Yahweh saves" or "salvation is from Yahweh." God named Jesus. He told Mary and Joseph what to name their baby. God also gave Jesus many other names. Here are some of Jesus' names.

| NAME | MEANING | BIBLE REFERENCE |
|---|---|---|
| Immanuel | God with us | Matthew 1:23 |
| Son of David | Brings in the Kingdom | Matthew 9:27 |
| Christ/Messiah | Anointed One of God | Matthew 16:16 |
| Son of Man | Divine title of suffering and exaltation | Matthew 20:28 |
| Word | Reveals God | John 1:1 |
| Lamb of God | Life sacrificed for sin | John 1:29 |
| Savior | Delivers from sin | John 4:42 |
| Good Shepherd | Gives guidance and protection | John 10:11 |
| Son of God | Jesus' unique relationship with God | John 20:31 |
| Lord | Sovereign Creator and Redeemer | Romans 10:9 |
| King of kings, Lord of lords | The Sovereign Almighty | Revelation 19:16 |
| Alpha and Omega | The Beginning and End of All Things | Revelation 21:6 |

The name *Jesus* is used over 900 times in the New Testament, but did you know every book in the Bible points to Jesus? Each day this week, you will discover more about the names of Jesus found in different books of the Bible.

# DAY 1

## THE BOOK OF MATTHEW

VERSE OF THE DAY: Matthew 1:23 / CHALLENGE: Isaiah 7:14

**DO!** Cross out all of the odd numbered letters. Write the remaining letters in order in the spaces below to discover one of Jesus' names.

| | | | |
|---|---|---|---|
| 2 I | 7 Z | 9 H | 8 M |
| 22 M | 14 A | 15 T | 21 I |
| 11 S | 35 B | 4 N | 42 U |
| 19 W | 38 E | 17 K | 29 O |
| 3 R | 13 U | 26 L | 47 N |

___ ___ ___ ___ ___ ___ ___ ___
2   8   22  14  4   42  38  26

When you feel lonely or bored, remember you are never alone. You can talk to Jesus or read about Him in the Bible anytime!

**KNOW!**

✓ *Immanuel* means "God with us."
✓ Find these names of Jesus in Matthew.
→ King of the Jews
   (Matthew 2:2; 27:37)
→ Nazarene (Matthew 2:23)
→ Prophet (Matthew 21:11)
→ Son of God (Matthew 26:63-65)
→ Son of David and Son of Abraham
   (Matthew 1:1)

**PRAY** Focus on the name *Immanuel*—God with us—in your prayer. Thank God for sending Jesus.

# DAY 2

## THE BOOK OF MARK

VERSE OF THE DAY: Mark 14:61 / CHALLENGE: 1 John 5:1

**DO!** In the blocks going down, write the name of each picture. Read the letters across the top of the blocks to discover another name Jesus is called.

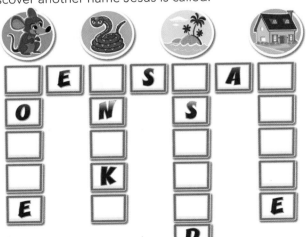

**KNOW!**

✓ *Messiah* means "anointed one" and is also translated as "Christ."
✓ Check out these names Jesus was called in the Book of Mark.
→ The Holy One of God (Mark 1:24)
→ Lord (Mark 1:3)
→ Shepherd (Mark 14:27)
→ Son of Man (Mark 2:28)
→ Teacher (Mark 5:35)

**PRAY** Praise Jesus for being the Messiah. Ask Him to help you tell people about Him.

## DAY 3

# THE BOOK OF LUKE

VERSE OF THE DAY: Luke 2:11
CHALLENGE: Romans 10:9-10

DO! Write the names of the three pictures, then remove the letters. Write the remaining letters on the blanks to learn today's name for Jesus.

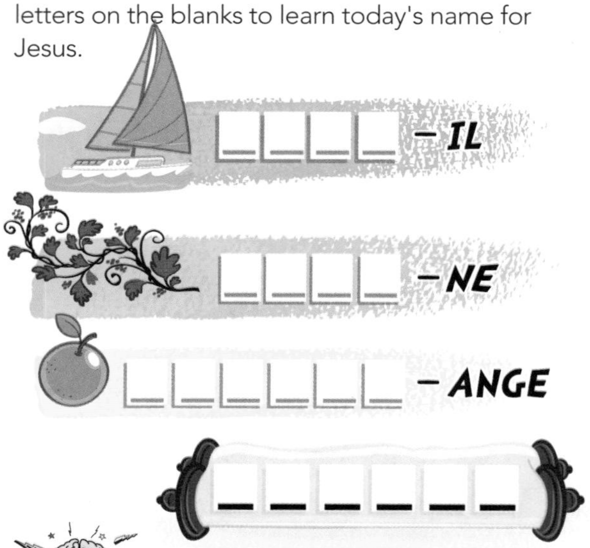

_ _ _ _ – IL

_ _ _ _ – NE

_ _ _ _ _ _ – ANGE

_ _ _ _ _ _

KNOW!

- Savior means "one who saves."
- In Old Testament times, God was called Savior.
- God sent His Son, Jesus, to save us from the sin that separates us from God.
- Through Jesus, we are able to have a relationship where we can pray and talk to God.
- Check out these names Jesus was called in the Book of Luke.
  - → God's Chosen One (Luke 23:35)
  - → Son of God (Luke 1:35)
  - → Son of the Most High (Luke 1:32)
  - → Son of David (Luke 18:39)
  - → Horn of Salvation (Luke 1:69)

PRAY Praise God for sending Jesus as our Savior.

## DAY 4

# THE BOOK OF JOHN

VERSE OF THE DAY: John 3:2
CHALLENGE: Colossians 3:16

DO! Write the opposite of each word. Then put the numbered letters in their correct spaces.

Front ___ ___ ___ ___ (3, 4)

Cold ___ ___ ___ (5, 1)

Early ___ ___ ___ ___ (2)

Enemy ___ ___ ___ ___ ___ ___ (7, 6)

___ ___ ___ ___ ___ ___ ___
1 2 3 4 5 6 7

? Who is your favorite teacher? Why?
? Write some things Jesus taught:

- ☆
- ☆
- ☆

KNOW!

- Jesus taught His followers to do what is right and good.
- You can be a teacher of good for those who watch you.
- Check out these names Jesus was called in the Book of John.
  - → Bread of Life (John 6:48)
  - → Lamb of God (John 1:29)
  - → Light of the World (John 8:12)
  - → Word (John 1:1)
  - → Way, truth, and life (John 14:6)
  - → Rabbi/Teacher (John 1:38)

PRAY Ask God to lead you to make right choices—in your talk and actions.

# DAY 5

## THE BOOK OF REVELATION

VERSE OF THE DAY: Revelation 1:17 / CHALLENGE: 1 Corinthians 15:45-49

**DO!** Complete the chart by filling in the "first" and "last" information for each category.

| CATEGORY | FIRST | LAST |
|---|---|---|
| Letters in the alphabet | | |
| Your name | | |
| Places you lived | | |
| Months of the year | | |
| Days of the week | | |
| Books of the Bible | | |
| Words in Book of Revelation | | |

**KNOW!**

✓ Jesus is called the "First and the Last" because He was present from the beginning of time (Genesis 1:26) and He will be with us forever.

✓ Jesus should also be the first and last person you go to for answers to your problems or decisions to make.

✓ Check out these names Jesus was called in the Book of Revelation:
→ Alpha and Omega, Beginning and the End (Revelation 1:8; 22:13)
→ Faithful and True (Revelation 19:11)
→ Lion from the Tribe of Judah (Revelation 5:5)
→ Amen (Revelation 3:14)
→ Bright Morning Star (Revelation 22:16)

**PRAY** Ask God to help you remember to seek His guidance first and last in your decisions.

---

# DAY 6

## IMPORTANCE OF A NAME

VERSE OF THE DAY: Ezekiel 36:23 / CHALLENGE: Psalm 145:2

**DO!** Write your name in fancy or large letters.

List 10 things about yourself that your friends might notice.

1

2

3

4

5

6

7

8

9

10

? Having trouble? Ask a parent or sibling.

? What do people think when your name is said? Do your friends think of *Christian, loves Jesus, good friend,* or *cares about and helps people*?

**KNOW!**

✓ You are identified by your name. Your name can bring fear, happy thoughts, or angry thoughts to people. How you behave and talk will be associated with your name.

✓ Isaiah 9:6 lists many names Jesus would be called one day. Jesus is still called by these names. The names bring peace, love, and comfort to people.

**PRAY** Pray that your name will bring happy thoughts and thoughts of Jesus to others.

# JESUS FACTS

Check out these facts about Jesus.

Jesus' great-great-great grandfather was Eliud (Matthew 1:15).

When Jesus died, saints (followers of Jesus) arose from the dead and walked around Jerusalem (Matthew 27:51-53).

Angels took care of Jesus after He was tempted by Satan (Matthew 4:11).

Jesus was arrested in an olive grove (John 18:1-3,12).

Jesus lived in Egypt for a while because Herod wanted to kill Him (Matthew 2:13).

Jesus appeared before Herod, the ruler who had John the Baptist beheaded (Luke 9:7-9; 23:7).

Jesus handed over John, His disciple, to His mother as a son (John 19:25-27).

Jesus lives in heaven at the right hand of God (Mark 16:19).

The name *Jesus* means "the Lord saves."

By spitting in the dirt, Jesus made mud to heal a blind man (John 9:6).

The shortest verse in the Bible is John 11:35. Write the verse here:

Jesus was probably 33 years old when He was crucified.

Jesus was never created—He has always existed (Micah 5:2).

Jesus had several half brothers and sisters (Matthew 12:46-47; 13:55-56).

Although we celebrate Jesus' birthday on December 25, we don't know His actual birthday.

The name *Jesus* appears in the Bible over 900 times.

Jesus is the same yesterday, today, and forever (Hebrews 13:8).

Jesus was a carpenter (Mark 6:3).

When Jesus was 12 years old, He spent a few days in Jerusalem without His parents (Luke 2:41-50).

Jesus is the Creator of everything (Colossians 1:16-17).

John the Baptist was Jesus' relative.

Jesus was probably about 30 years old when He was baptized by John the Baptist.

Jesus is 100% God and 100% human.

How many facts did you already know?

How many were new to you?

# JESUS: HIS TRIUMPHAL ENTRY AND LAST SUPPER

BILL EMEOTT

On the Sunday before Jesus was crucified on Friday, Jesus entered Jerusalem. Jesus sent two of His disciples ahead to prepare for His entrance into town. Jesus told the disciples where they could find a donkey and her colt. This fulfilled the Old Testament prophecy found in Zechariah 9:9. The disciples brought Jesus the donkey and colt as He had instructed them. They spread robes on the animals and Jesus sat on the colt and began His ride into town.

A large crowd came to see Jesus because of His teachings and miracles. Some people spread their robes on the ground to acknowledge Jesus' royalty. Others cut branches and laid them on the ground as an act of recognizing Jesus as a king.

The followers began shouting, "Hosanna!" and "Blessed is He who comes in the name of the Lord!" indicating they believed Jesus was the saving Messiah. They thought Jesus—the Messiah—would sit on an earthly throne; they didn't imagine He would die on a cross instead.

Because the religious leaders were pretty upset with what was happening, they began to develop a plan to put Jesus to death. This same week, the Jews were celebrating Passover—a time of remembering and celebrating what God had done for the Israelites when He delivered them from Egyptian slavery. Jesus and His disciples were Jewish and they participated in this celebration.

On Thursday night, the disciples gathered to share the traditional Passover feast. Jesus instructed two of the disciples to prepare the meal in an upstairs room of a certain house in Jerusalem. Jesus knew that His time with the disciples would soon be over and He would be arrested, put on trial, and killed. We often call this meal "The Last Supper" because it would be the last meal Jesus would eat before he died.

At the time, the disciples did not understand everything Jesus said. He told them the bread should remind them of His body that would be given. The drink symbolized Jesus' blood that would be shed on the cross. Jesus told them to have this special meal again to remember what He was about to do for all people. Churches today choose different ways to observe this special meal. Some call it the "Lord's Supper" and some call it "Communion." The important thing is that we observe this meal and remember what Jesus did for us.

As you focus on the Triumphal Entry and the Last Supper this week, look for new things God wants to teach you!

## DAY 1 — JESUS CHOSE

VERSES OF THE DAY: Matthew 21:1-5
CHALLENGE: Ephesians 5:2

 Place a check by the statements you sometimes choose to do:

☐ Sometimes I choose to throw trash on the ground. _____

☐ Sometimes I choose to not tell the truth.
_____

☐ Sometimes I choose to be mean to a friend.
_____

☐ Sometimes I choose to disobey my parents.
_____

☐ Sometimes I choose to use language that is not nice. _____

On the line, write what God would have you do in that circumstance.

**KNOW!**

√ Even though it was difficult, Jesus freely chose to follow God's plan that would lead Him to Jerusalem where He would be killed.
√ You should choose to do what God tells you to do, even when it's difficult.
√ You can know God will help you make the right choices.

**PRAY** Thank Jesus for choosing to follow God's plan and paying the penalty for your sins. Ask God to help you make choices that are pleasing to Him.

## DAY 2 — ROBES AND BRANCHES

VERSES OF THE DAY: Matthew 21:6-8
CHALLENGE: Proverbs 3:9

 List some of your favorite things:

| MY FAVORITE THINGS | HONORING JESUS |
|---|---|
| | |
| | |
| | |
| | |

**?** How can you use these things to honor Jesus?

**KNOW!**

√ When Jesus entered Jerusalem, the people honored Him by lining His path with their outer robes and palm branches.
√ Palm trees were considered valuable. They provided food (dates, coconuts, coconut milk), fiber (for baskets, mats, and cooking utensils), medicines, and even fine perfume.
√ Spreading palm leaves and branches on Jesus' path meant the people honored Jesus with something of great value.
√ Just as the people honored Jesus with their valuables, you can honor Jesus with your things too.

**PRAY** Ask God to help you honor Him with your actions and the things you have been given.

## DAY 3

### HOSANNA TO THE KING!

VERSES OF THE DAY: Matthew 21:9-11 / CHALLENGE: Psalm 100:1

**DO!** Write inside the letters of Jesus' name words and phrases that honor Him:

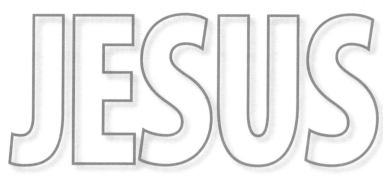

**KNOW!**

✓ The Bible teaches us we must confess Jesus is Savior and Lord.

✓ *Hosanna* means "save now!"

✓ The Jewish people shouted "Hosanna" and proclaimed that Jesus "comes in the name of the Lord." Some believed Jesus was the Messiah, but most didn't understand what that really meant.

✓ As a Christian, you can know Jesus truly is Savior and Lord.

**PRAY** Thank God for sending Jesus to save us from our sins.

## DAY 4

### THE FIRST LORD'S SUPPER

VERSES OF THE DAY: Matthew 26:17-20 / CHALLENGE: Psalm 69:30

**DO!** Complete the following sentences:

My favorite food is ...

My favorite holiday is ...

My favorite family tradition is ...

My favorite Bible story is ...

My favorite memory is ...

**KNOW!**

✓ The Passover is a tradition in the Jewish faith. The celebration includes a meal to remind the people how God delivered the Jews from Egyptian slavery.

✓ Jesus and His disciples were celebrating the Passover meal when Jesus instructed them to remember what He would soon do to deliver people from their sins.

✓ Some people refer to this meal as "The Last Supper," but Christians can know that it was also the first "Lord's Supper."

✓ You can remember that Jesus died on the cross for your sins when you participate in the Lord's Supper with your church.

**PRAY** Thank God for providing Jesus to save you from your sins.

## DAY 5

### THE BODY AND THE BLOOD

VERSES OF THE DAY: Matthew 26:26-29
CHALLENGE: 1 Chronicles 16:34

 Draw a picture of what you think the Last Supper might have looked like.

**KNOW!**

✓ Flat bread and wine are both part of the traditional Passover meal.
✓ Flat bread reminded the Jewish people they left Egypt so quickly they didn't have time to add yeast to their dough.
✓ Wine reminded the Jewish people of animal sacrifices that were required for forgiveness of people's sins.
✓ Jesus took these symbolic Passover foods and gave them new symbolic meaning.
✓ Only Christians should participate in the Lord's Supper.
✓ When you participate in the Lord's Supper you should be reminded of Jesus' body that was given and His blood that was shed on the cross for your sins.

**PRAY** Thank Jesus for giving His body and shedding His blood for your sins.

## DAY 6

### DON'T FORGET TO SING!

VERSE OF THE DAY: Matthew 26:30
CHALLENGE: Psalm 147:1

 List your favorite praise songs you sing at church:

Consider organizing a small group of family members or friends to sing these songs of praise for other family members, friends, or people who need encouragement.

**KNOW!**

✓ After the Last Supper, the disciples sang, then left the room, and went to the garden with Jesus.
✓ Singing is often a reflection of an attitude of thankfulness and happiness.
✓ Christians should be happy and thankful when remembering what Jesus did for them on the cross.
✓ Our actions should reflect our thankfulness.

**PRAY** Sing a praise song to Jesus as a prayer of thankfulness and love for what He has done for you.

# HOSANNA!

Have you ever seen signs and posters people hold up at sporting events to cheer their teams? That's similar to what the people were doing when they waved palm branches and shouted, "Hosanna!" as Jesus made His way into Jerusalem. The people were praising Jesus and worshiping Him.

Design a sign or poster you could use to praise and worship Jesus.

# CRACK THE CODE

Use the code below to decode the words on the page.

<u>2</u> <u>5</u> <u>17</u> <u>22</u> <u>1</u> <u>14</u> <u>1</u> <u>16</u> <u>18</u> <u>6</u>

are commands or rules that . . .

were begun by Jesus.
were taught by the disciples.
were practiced by the early church.
are not required for salvation.

<u>23</u> <u>18</u> <u>6</u> <u>8</u> <u>6</u> told us to observe the <u>2</u> <u>5</u> <u>17</u> <u>22</u> <u>1</u> <u>14</u> <u>1</u> <u>16</u> <u>18</u> <u>6</u> of

<u>15</u> <u>14</u> <u>3</u> <u>7</u> <u>22</u> <u>6</u> <u>26</u> and <u>7</u> <u>21</u> <u>18</u> <u>25</u> <u>2</u> <u>5</u> <u>17</u> <u>6</u>

<u>6</u> <u>8</u> <u>3</u> <u>3</u> <u>18</u> <u>5</u> with <u>2</u> <u>7</u> <u>21</u> <u>18</u> <u>5</u>

<u>16</u> <u>21</u> <u>5</u> <u>22</u> <u>6</u> <u>7</u> <u>22</u> <u>14</u> <u>1</u> <u>6</u>

We observe these <u>2</u> <u>5</u> <u>17</u> <u>22</u> <u>1</u> <u>14</u> <u>1</u> <u>16</u> <u>18</u> <u>6</u> in our churches today.

Read Matthew 28:18-20 to find out what <u>23</u> <u>18</u> <u>6</u> <u>8</u> <u>6</u> said about

<u>15</u> <u>14</u> <u>3</u> <u>7</u> <u>22</u> <u>6</u> <u>26</u>

WRITE THE VERSES HERE:

Read Luke 22:19 to find out what <u>23</u> <u>18</u> <u>6</u> <u>8</u> <u>6</u> said about

<u>7</u> <u>21</u> <u>18</u> <u>25</u> <u>2</u> <u>5</u> <u>17</u> <u>6</u> <u>6</u> <u>8</u> <u>3</u> <u>3</u> <u>18</u> <u>5</u>

WRITE THE VERSE HERE:

# JESUS: HIS FRIENDS AND ENEMIES

WILLIAM SUMMEY

Last week you read about Jesus' journey into Jerusalem. So many people cheered and worshiped Jesus, but many people were not happy to see how the crowd praised Jesus. Many leaders in Jerusalem were so upset they wanted to kill Jesus! One of Jesus' disciples, Judas Iscariot, betrayed Jesus with a kiss, showing the guards who Jesus was so He could be arrested. These are some of the reasons people wanted to hurt Jesus:

- The leaders were jealous. They saw how the people loved Jesus. The leaders wanted people to say good things about them.
- The leaders were angry. They did not like how Jesus told them they were wrong. Jesus told the leaders things they did not understand about the Scriptures.
- The leaders were afraid people would stop listening to them. They did not like that the people started to listen to Jesus more.
- The leaders would not listen to God. Jesus told how they sinned. Instead of turning back to God, the leaders were stubborn. They refused to believe Jesus' words and actions and what the prophets had said about Jesus.
- Judas loved money more than Jesus. One of the Ten Commandments is about not making idols. An idol is not just a little statue. An idol is anything you put in place of God or think about more than God. Judas put money ahead of following Jesus.

Many people loved Jesus and would do anything for Him. The Bible even tells of one woman who honored Jesus in a very special way. She seemed to understand that Jesus was going to die soon. She poured special oil that cost a lot of money on Jesus. Jesus was very pleased that she honored Him in that way. Jesus even told her she would always be remembered because of this kind action (Matthew 26:7-13).

What are some ways you can honor Jesus today? You don't have Jesus with you in the way the disciples did, but you can still show Jesus how you love Him. Try the following:

- Pray, thanking Jesus for loving you and making a way you can spend forever in heaven with Him.
- Read your Bible. God has so much to teach you in the Bible.
- Give and serve. God wants you to help others. You can give your money, your time, and help people who are in trouble.
- Tell others about Jesus. Tell your friends, classmates, neighbors, and anyone you meet about Jesus, even those you consider enemies.
- Forgive people who have hurt you. This is so hard to do, but this is what Jesus did. If you forgive, you help show people the love of God.

Can you think of other ways you can show Jesus you love Him?

# DAY 1

## THE PLAN AGAINST JESUS

VERSES OF THE DAY: Matthew 26:3-4 / CHALLENGE: Matthew 26:1-5

**DO!** Have you ever been accused of doing something you didn't do? What was it? How did you feel?

Connect the red dots below to find the hidden message.

Jesus never sinned. Jesus is …

**KNOW!**

✓ Jesus never sinned (Hebrews 4:15).

✓ Jesus was accused of things that were not true (Matthew 26:59).

✓ Jesus was willing to forgive the people who wanted to hurt Him (Luke 23:34).

**PRAY** Ask God to help you live like Jesus. Thank Him for forgiving you when you fail.

# DAY 2

## GIVE YOUR BEST

VERSES OF THE DAY: Matthew 26:6-7 / CHALLENGE: Matthew 26:6-11

**DO!** Circle all the things you can give to God or do for Him.

**?** What other things can you give to God? Include not just things you can give, but things you can do.

**?** Why is giving God your best the right thing to do?

**KNOW!**

✓ God says He wants the best for us (Jeremiah 29:11).

✓ The woman in today's story gave Jesus a very expensive gift (John 12:3-5).

✓ We can give God more than things (John 14:15).

✓ We can give God our love, talents, and time (Colossians 3:17).

✓ Everything we own belongs to God (Psalm 24:1).

**PRAY** Ask God to help you always give Him your very best.

# DAY 3

## SHOW AND TELL

VERSE OF THE DAY: Matthew 26:13
CHALLENGE: Matthew 26:12-16

**DO!** Look at this illustration of what Carlee brought to "Show and Tell" at school. Make up a crazy story about what Carlee said and tell it to a friend.

Act out the following words for family members without saying anything. See if anyone can guess the word. Read the "Challenge" verses to find ways some of these words are used in the Bible.

**CHURCH**

**OIL**

**LOVE**

**FRIEND**

**MONEY**

**BURIAL**

**GIVE**

**KNOW!**

✓ You show people you love Jesus when you do good things (James 1:22).
✓ You show people you love Jesus when you love others (John 13:35).
✓ You tell people about Jesus when sharing how you became a Christian (1 Corinthians 15:3-8).

**PRAY** Ask God to help you show other people you love God by what you do and say.

# DAY 4

## OBEY GOD

VERSES OF THE DAY: Matthew 26:18-19
CHALLENGE: Matthew 26:17-25

**DO!** Write the names of people who are important for you to obey.

? Did you include teacher, doctor, parent, police officer, firefighter, or coach?
? Why is it important to obey the people you put on your list?

**KNOW!**

✓ God wants us to obey Him (1 John 5:3).
✓ God says if we love Him, we will obey Him (John 14:15).
✓ God is pleased when we obey (Colossians 3:20).
✓ God corrects us when we do not obey (Proverbs 3:12).
✓ God is always willing to forgive when we ask (1 John 1:9).

**PRAY** Ask God to help you obey Him and the important people He puts in your life.

## DAY 5 — PRAY FOR HELP

VERSE OF THE DAY: Matthew 26:36 / CHALLENGE: Matthew 26:36-46

**DO!** Draw a picture of someone who needs help.

? What could you do to help the person you drew?

? How could prayer help the person?

 **KNOW!**

✓ God hears us when we pray (1 John 5:14).
✓ God wants us to ask Him for help (James 1:5).
✓ God always answers prayer (Psalm 17:6).
✓ God sometimes says no to what we ask for (2 Corinthians 12:8-9).
✓ God promises to help (Isaiah 41:10).

**PRAY** Thank God that He helps you when you need it! Ask Him to show you how you can help people in need.

## DAY 6 — WHEN OTHERS HURT US

VERSES OF THE DAY: Matthew 26:50,69-70 / CHALLENGE: Matthew 26:47-56,69-75

**DO!** How do you feel when a friend hurts you? Touch your finger on the square that describes how you feel.

MAD    HURT

AFRAID    SAD

How do you think Jesus felt when Judas hurt Him by betraying Him? Touch your finger on the square that describes how you think Jesus felt.

How do you think Jesus felt when Peter hurt Him by denying he knew Him? Touch your finger on the square that describes how you think Jesus felt.

 **KNOW!**

✓ God promises never to leave us or forsake us (Deuteronomy 31:6).
✓ People will let us down and hurt us sometimes, but God will not (Deuteronomy 31:8).
✓ We can choose to forgive people who hurt us (Mark 11:25).

**PRAY** Ask God to help you love those who hurt you.

# ACTION-PEOPLE MATCH

Read each clue from Matthew 26. When you know which person the clue is talking about, touch that person's name. For extra fun, have someone call these out to you to see how fast you can answer each clue.

Took 30 pieces of silver from those wanting to hurt Jesus

Said "Wherever the gospel is told, what this woman has done will be remembered."

Tried to protect Jesus with a sword

Brought a jar of expensive oil

**Peter**

**Judas**

Told Peter, "Tonight before the rooster crows you will deny Me three times."

Said "I will never run away!"

Poured oil on Jesus

Betrayed Jesus with a kiss

**Woman**

**Jesus**

 **CHALLENGE CLUE**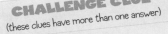
(these clues have more than one answer)

Was a disciple of Jesus

Visited the home of Simon

Ate together at the Last Supper

Was willing to suffer because of His great love for you and me

# DIG DEEPER!

Why did the woman in Matthew 26 pour oil on Jesus' head?

Read the following facts to find out some of the reasons.

*Anoint* means "to pour or rub oil to set apart, heal, or prepare for burial."

Jesus is King of kings. Oil was often used to anoint kings. God sent Samuel to anoint King David in 1 Samuel 16:1. At the Triumphal Entry, people cheered Jesus like a king. The woman in Matthew 26 anointed Jesus' head like a king. The angel told Mary before Jesus' birth how long Jesus' kingdom would last. Read Luke 1:33 to find out and write your answer here:

Jesus' kingdom will _____.

Jesus is the Messiah, or Christ, which also means "anointed one" (Matthew 16:16). This literally means that Jesus was set apart for a specific task. What was His task? Read John 3:16 to find out!

Why did God send Jesus? _____

Jesus knew He was going to die later that week. He said that this woman was preparing His body for burial. Read Matthew 26:13 to find out how important this was to Jesus.

Wherever the gospel is shared what this woman did will be _____.

Read John 12:1-11 and discover both the name of the woman who anointed Jesus with oil and how much the oil was worth. Write your answers here:

The woman's name was _____.

The oil was worth _____.

Pray, asking God how you can honor Him this week.

Look at the bottom of page 74 for some ideas.

# JESUS: ON TRIAL

GORDON BROWN

"Hey! That's not fair!" Have you ever said that—maybe when someone jumps to the front of the line—or cheats on the playground? Sometimes things are just not fair. For example:

- Is it fair if someone makes your words sound like a lie?
- Is it fair to be punished for something that wasn't your fault?
- Is it fair if someone hits you or slaps you because they disagree with what you said?
- Is it fair to be called names or have bad things said about you when you've done nothing wrong?
- Is it fair if your best friends pretend like they don't even know you?

None of these things are fair, but all of them happened to Jesus. He could have said, "Hey! That's not fair!" but He didn't. Instead, Jesus said nothing at all. He remained silent.

Jesus was taken to the home of Caiaphas, the high priest (or leader), where the Sanhedrin (a group of teachers and rulers of the Jewish temple) had gathered. Meeting at night, so no one would know, Caiaphas and the Sanhedrin were looking for a way to have Jesus put to death even though He was innocent of any crime. The Sanhedrin did not believe what Jesus taught was true. They were angry that people believed Jesus was the Son of God. They were so angry they wanted to kill Jesus and looked for others to agree with them. They eventually found two people willing to be false witnesses. (A *false witness* is "someone who doesn't tell the truth.") The two false witnesses told the Sanhedrin what they wanted to hear by making Jesus' words sound like a lie.

The story gets even worse. During the trial, some people asked Peter if Jesus was his friend. Peter—one of Jesus' disciples and friends—said no. Not just one time but three times! Jesus knew Peter would do this. Jesus also knew the trial wouldn't be fair. Why didn't He say anything? Why did Jesus let them treat Him so unfairly? Why was Jesus being punished for something He didn't do?

Jesus did all of this because it was part of God's plan. He did it because He loves His Father. He did it because He loves us. He was innocent, yet He was punished for our sins. The way Jesus was treated wasn't fair, but He did it anyway.

You can read the whole story in Matthew 26:57–27:31. As you complete the daily activities this week, you'll discover attitudes and actions that helped Jesus endure His trial.

## DAY 1 — OBEY

VERSE OF THE DAY: Hebrews 5:8
CHALLENGE: Matthew 26:57-68

 Color the numbers with the matching color. A picture will appear when you're done!

**1** Blue **2** Purple **3** Green **4** Yellow **5** Pink

```
1 1 1 1 1 1 1 1 1 1 1 1 1 1 1 1 1 4 1 1 1 1 1 1 1 1
1 1 1 1 1 1 1 1 1 1 1 1 1 1 1 1 1 4 1 1 1 1 1 1 1 1
1 1 1 5 5 1 1 1 1 1 1 1 1 1 1 1 4 1 1 1 1 1 1 1 1 1
1 5 5 5 5 5 1 5 5 1 1 1 1 4 1 1 1 1 1 1 1 1 1 1 4 1
5 5 5 5 5 5 5 5 5 1 1 1 1 4 1 1 1 1 1 1 1 1 1 4 1
1 5 5 1 1 1 1 1 1 1 1 1 4 4 1 4 4 4 4 4 1 1 1 4 1 1
1 1 1 1 1 1 1 1 1 1 4 1 4 4 4 4 4 4 4 4 4 1 1 4 1
1 1 1 1 1 1 1 1 1 1 1 4 1 4 4 4 4 4 4 4 4 1 1 1 1
1 1 1 1 3 1 1 1 1 1 1 1 1 4 4 4 4 4 1 1 5 5 5 1
1 1 3 3 3 1 1 1 2 2 2 2 2 1 1 4 4 4 4 4 1 1 5 5 5 5
1 1 3 3 3 1 1 2 2 2 2 2 2 2 2 1 1 4 1 1 1 5 5 5 5
1 3 3 3 3 3 2 2 2 2 2 2 2 2 2 4 1 1 4 1 1 5 5 5 5
1 3 3 3 3 2 2 2 2 2 2 2 2 2 2 2 1 1 1 1 1 1 1 1 1
1 3 3 3 3 3 2 2 2 2 2 2 2 2 2 2 2 2 1 1 1 1 1 1 1
1 3 3 3 3 3 3 2 2 2 2 2 2 2 2 2 2 2 1 1 1 1 1 1 1
1 3 3 3 3 3 2 2 2 2 2 2 2 2 2 2 2 2 1 1 1 1 1 1 1
1 1 3 1 2 3 2 2 2 2 2 2 2 2 2 2 2 2 2 2 2 1 2
3 3 1 3 3 2 2 2 2 2 2 2 2 2 2 2 2 2 2 2 2 2
3 3 3 3 3 3 2 2 2 3 2 2 2 2 2 2 2 2 2 2 2 2
3 3 3 3 3 3 3 3 3 3 3 3 3 3 3 3 3 3 3 3 2 2 2
3 3 3 3 3 3 3 3 3 3 3 3 3 3 3 3 3 3 3 3 3 3 2 2
3 3 3 3 3 3 3 3 3 3 3 3 3 3 3 3 3 3 3 3 3 3 3 3
3 3 3 3 3 3 3 3 3 3 3 3 3 3 3 3 3 3 3 3 3 3 3 3
3 3 3 3 3 3 3 3 3 3 3 3 3 3 3 3 3 3 3 3 3 3 3 3
3 3 3 3 3 3 3 3 3 3 3 3 3 3 3 3 3 3 3 3 3 3 3 3
3 3 3 3 3 3 3 3 3 3 3 3 3 3 3 3 3 3 3 3 3 3 3 3
3 3 3 3 3 3 3 3 3 3 3 3 3 3 3 3 3 3 3 3 3 3 3 3
```

✓ Jesus obeyed His Father. Obeying God helps you become more like Jesus.
✓ God can see what we cannot see.
✓ God will take care of you.
✓ You show God you love Him when you obey His commands (1 John 5:3).
✓ The Holy Spirit gives you the power to obey.

**PRAY** Ask God to help you obey even when you cannot see His plan.

## DAY 2 — TRUST

VERSES OF THE DAY: Proverbs 3:5-6
CHALLENGE: Matthew 26:69-75

 Scribble art. Make these scribbles into a picture.

✓ Jesus trusted God even when He was afraid (Matthew 26:39).
✓ When you are afraid, you can trust in God.
✓ God knows what He is doing.
✓ God can make something beautiful out of a big mess.
✓ God sees and knows everything.
✓ God is always with you.
✓ Even the darkness is not dark to God (Psalm 139:12).

**PRAY** Ask God to help you trust Him when you are afraid and don't understand. Thank Him for turning messes into something beautiful.

## DAY 3

# DON'T GIVE UP

VERSE OF THE DAY: John 16:33 / CHALLENGE: Matthew 27:1-10

 Unscramble the following word.

# DEUQOCERN

_____ _ _ _ _ _ _ _ _

**HINT:** You can find the word used in John 16:33 in some Bible translations. The word means "overcame."

After you figure the word out, see how many other words you can make by rearranging the letters. The words in your list must have at least three letters each. Don't give up until you've come up with at least five new words!

_____  _____

_____  _____

_____  _____

_____  _____

**KNOW!**

✓ Jesus did not give up even when He was being treated unfairly.
✓ God will encourage you when you want to give up.
✓ When you are weak, God is strong.
✓ God is with you wherever you go.
✓ Since God is for us, no one can be against us (Romans 8:31).

**PRAY** Ask God for strength and courage when you are weak and afraid.

## DAY 4

# REST

DAILY VERSE: Matthew 11:28 / CHALLENGE: Matthew 27:11-14

**DO!** What's different? Look at the picture on the left. Can you find 10 things different in the picture on the right?

**KNOW!**

✓ Jesus knew God would take care of Him.
✓ God will take care of you.
✓ God is in control.
✓ God is good all the time!
✓ God is always with you.
✓ God holds you in the palm of His hand (John 10:28).

**PRAY** Ask God to help you rest even when you are worried or afraid.

# DAY 5 — GIVE THANKS

VERSE OF THE DAY: 1 Thessalonians 5:18
CHALLENGE: Matthew 27:15-26

**DO!** Being thankful when things do not go your way is tough to do. Can you think of something to be thankful for (good or bad) that begins with each letter of the alphabet? Find a friend and take turns. You might be surprised what she says she's thankful for!

a _____    n _____
b _____    o _____
c _____    p _____
d _____    q _____
e _____    r _____
f _____    s _____
g _____    t _____
h _____    u _____
i _____    v _____
j _____    w _____
k _____    x _____
l _____    y _____
m _____    z _____

**KNOW!**

✓ Because Jesus was following God's perfect plan, He could be thankful.
✓ God's peace will guard your heart and mind.
✓ God wants you to be honest with Him when you pray.
✓ God doesn't want you to worry.
✓ God can turn your sadness to joy.

**PRAY** Ask God to help you be thankful, even when it is difficult and you feel like there is nothing to be thankful for.

# DAY 6 — HAVE HOPE

VERSE OF THE DAY: Jeremiah 29:11
CHALLENGE: Matthew 27:27-31

**DO!** Begin at the "Start" of the maze. Follow the path to the "Finish." When you're done, you'll discover the maze reveals a picture!

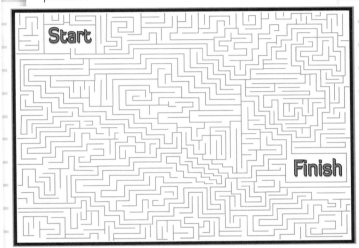

**KNOW!**

✓ Because Jesus was following God's perfect plan, He could have hope.
✓ God can see what you cannot see.
✓ God's way is perfect (Psalm 18:30).
✓ God gave His own Son for you. He will not lead you the wrong way.
✓ God has a good plan for your life.
✓ God always loves you, even during hard times.
✓ God will go with you wherever you go and will always watch over you (Genesis 28:15).

**PRAY** Ask God to help you follow His path. (You may not understand until you reach the end and can see what God sees—the big picture!)

# WHO'S WHO?

Many people played a part in Jesus' trial. Draw a line from each description on the left to the matching picture. If you need help, search Matthew 26:57–27:31.

● Barabbas

● Sanhedrin

● Judas

Person on trial; the Son of God

High priest; leader of the Sanhedrin

Disciple who denied knowing Jesus

Group of teachers and rulers of the Jewish church

Governor who found Jesus guilty of nothing

Disciple who betrayed Jesus; hanged himself

Prisoner released instead of Jesus

Group who shouted, "Crucify Him!"

Group who mocked Jesus; led Jesus away to be crucified

● Jesus

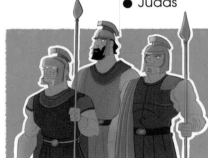

● Soldiers

● Peter

● Caiaphas

● Pilate

● Crowd

# CHALLENGE ACTIVITY

Search Matthew 26:57–27:31 and write the verses where you read about the people.
The first one is done for you.

Jesus: Matthew 26:57,62–64; Matthew 27:1–2,11–14,26–31

Caiaphas: _____

Peter: _____

Sanhedrin: _____

Pilate: _____

Judas: _____

Barabbas: _____

Crowd: _____

Soldiers: _____

## FIND THE NAMES LISTED ABOVE IN THE PUZZLE.

```
E  O  H  S  S  V  B  V  N  H  I  C
T  K  U  A  P  R  S  J  G  D  A  L
A  C  E  N  E  U  E  Z  U  I  N  N
L  R  Q  H  S  H  P  I  A  D  L  N
I  O  P  E  T  E  R  P  D  O  A  C
P  W  J  D  G  L  H  D  V  L  B  S
H  D  G  R  U  A  N  F  N  A  O  Z
U  J  B  I  S  J  H  X  J  Y  N  S
A  C  S  N  S  A  B  B  A  R  A  B
```

# JESUS: CRUCIFIED ON A CROSS

HENRY DUTTON

From the very beginning of time, God had a plan to save people from sin and death. God planned a special rescue mission, and He sent His only Son, Jesus, to be our Savior. Over the past several weeks, you've learned about the birth and life of Jesus. This week, spend time reading and learning more about Jesus' death on the cross.

## Why Did Jesus Die?

The Bible teaches us that all humans sin (Romans 3:23). We all do things that break God's laws and make Him angry. The punishment for our sin is death and separation from God forever (Romans 6:23). Since we all sin, we all deserve this punishment, and that's bad news.

Jesus is 100 percent man, but He is also 100 percent God. When Jesus came to earth, He lived a perfect life. He never sinned or broke God's laws—not even once! Remember, the punishment for sin is death and separation from God, but since Jesus never sinned, He did not deserve to be punished.

Jesus loves us so much He died on the cross and took the punishment we deserve (Romans 5:8). We deserve death, but Jesus did not. He died in our place as our substitute. This is the greatest love anyone could ever show for us (John 15:13).

Because of Jesus, we can have life instead of death. We can live forever as God's people, and that's good news!

## No More Separation

In the Bible, the Jewish temple was divided into two parts by a thick curtain. On one side of the curtain was the sanctuary, and on the other side was the holy of holies. The holy of holies was a special place that represented God's presence on earth. So in the temple, the curtain separated sinful people from the holy God.

When Jesus died on the cross, the Bible tells us the thick curtain in the temple was torn from top to bottom (Matthew 27:51). This was God's way of showing us there is no more separation between God and man. All the things that separate us from God, like sin and death, were destroyed because of Jesus' perfect life and death on the cross.

Before Jesus came, only the high priest could go into the holy of holies in God's presence to make sacrifices and talk to God on behalf of all the people. Now, because of Jesus, we have the right to be called God's children, and we can talk to Him and spend time with Him anytime we want! That's good news too!

## LIVE FOR HIM

VERSE OF THE DAY: Mark 8:34 / CHALLENGE: Matthew 27:32-37

 What is the heaviest thing you can lift?
Ask permission, then go around your house and try to lift some of these things:

**Kitchen table**

**Bed**

**Couch**

**Dresser**

→ Were you able to lift these things? Now, imagine trying to carry one of these heavy things on your back like a backpack. Do you think you could do it?

→ On His way to be crucified, Jesus was forced to carry a heavy part of the cross on His back—the crossbeam. A man named Simon helped Jesus carry the crossbeam when He could not carry it any further.

✓ Jesus said we should take up our cross and follow Him. He does not actually want us to carry around a cross. This was His way of telling us we should live our lives only for Him.

✓ You can live for God by making good choices, reading and obeying His Word (the Bible), and telling others about Him.

**PRAY** Thank Jesus for dying on the cross. Ask Him to help you make good choices and to live only for Him.

## JESUS KNOWS AND CARES

VERSES OF THE DAY: Hebrews 4:15-16 / CHALLENGE: Matthew 27:38-44

 Have you ever been teased, bullied, or made fun of? When Jesus was on the cross, the people around Him made fun of Him and mocked Him. When people make fun of you, remember you are God's special creation. He made you exactly the way He wants you to be.

Ask permission, then grab a dry-erase marker. Now, look at yourself in the mirror, and write things that are special about you on the mirror next to your reflection.

✓ Jesus is fully God, but He is also fully human.

✓ The Bible says Jesus sympathizes with you (Hebrews 4:15-16). He understands all the things you go through in life and He wants to help you.

✓ You can talk to Jesus and read the Bible when things bother you.

 **PRAY** Thank God for making you exactly the way He wants you to be. Thank Jesus that He is always present for you when things are good and bad.

## TORN IN TWO

VERSE OF THE DAY: Matthew 27:51
CHALLENGE: Matthew 27:45-53

 Ask an adult for an old phone book. Try to rip the phone book in half from the side with the binding. Were you able to rip the phone book?

When Jesus died, the curtain in the temple was torn from top to bottom. This curtain was very thick— about four inches!—and would have been very difficult for a person to rip.

**KNOW!**

✓ When Jesus died, He destroyed all the things that separate you from God, like sin and death.

✓ When you ask Jesus to become your Savior and Lord, you can know you belong to God forever.

✓ After you become a Christian, you will still make mistakes and sin. Sin can hurt or damage your relationship with Jesus and cause you not to feel very close to Him.

✓ Jesus does not want anything to come between you and your relationship with Him.

**PRAY** Ask God to help you not sin. Ask Him to help you think of anything that might come between you and your relationship with Him so you can make changes in your life.

---

## WHO DO YOU SAY HE IS?

VERSE OF THE DAY: Matthew 27:54
CHALLENGE: Matthew 16:13-16

 Ask three people this question: "Who is Jesus?" Challenge them to answer in only one sentence. Write down what they say. Now, ask yourself the same question and write down your answer too.

**WHO IS JESUS?**

1.

2.

3.

My answer:

**KNOW!**

✓ When Jesus died on the cross, the guards who were watching over Him realized that Jesus truly is God's Son.

✓ People today believe many different things about Jesus. Some people say He was an ordinary man, and some say He was only a good teacher. Some people even say that Jesus did not exist.

✓ You can trust God's Word and believe that Jesus is both fully God and fully man.

**PRAY** Ask God to help you have courage to tell others Jesus is God's Son and He can save them from sin and death.

---

## DAY 5

# A NEW LIFE

VERSE OF THE DAY: Romans 6:4 / CHALLENGE: Matthew 27:55-61

**DO!** Draw a picture below of what you think Jesus' tomb might have looked like.

[                                                        ]

Did you know baptism is a symbol of Jesus' burial and resurrection? Ask an adult to show you the baptistry the next time you are at church.

✓ We deserve death and separation from God because of our sin, but because Jesus died in our place and rose again, we can have life instead of death.

✓ Baptism is a symbol. When someone goes into the water, it represents going into a tomb or grave. When someone comes out of the water, it represents coming out of the grave and having a new life.

✓ Baptism helps us celebrate the new life we have because of Jesus. Baptism also shows other people we want to live for Jesus.

**PRAY** Thank God for giving you life instead of death. Ask Him to help you live for Him and tell others about Him.

## DAY 6

# SEALED AND GUARDED

VERSE OF THE DAY: Matthew 27:66 / CHALLENGE: Matthew 27:62-66

**DO!** Try to sneak past someone, or right up next to her, without her noticing. Were you able to do it?

What things might give away someone trying to sneak up on you? Check all that apply:

☐ squeaky floor
☐ giggles
☐ reflection in glass
☐ smell of food they're holding

☐ bump into you
☐ noisy clothes
other: _____
other: _____

When Jesus was put in the tomb, a group of Roman soldiers guarded it, and no one could have sneaked past them.

✓ Because people remembered Jesus said He would rise again after three days, soldiers rolled a very large, heavy stone in front of the entrance to Jesus' tomb.

✓ People were afraid Jesus' disciples would steal His body from the tomb and claim He had been raised from the dead.

✓ Soldiers sealed and guarded Jesus' tomb. No person could open it.

**PRAY** Thank Jesus for His willingness to die in your place.

# CRUCIFIXION FACTS

Sometimes a sign was hung from the person's neck that described his crime, and then was attached to the cross.

Crucifixion had become a common form of punishment in Jesus' day.

Usually before a person was crucified, he would be beaten. Sometimes a whip that had pieces of bone or metal tied to the end was used. This beating was done to make the person die more quickly once he was on the cross.

After the person was beaten, he was forced to carry the crossbeam of the cross to the place he would be put to death. The crossbeam would have weighed about 100 pounds.

**crossbeam**

**pole**

**block of wood**

Crucifixions were usually done
side the city in public places, and bodies were often
left hanging for days.

People were usually
crucified without any clothes on,
so it was a humiliating death. Crucifixion
was also a very painful death. People who were
crucified usually died from loss of blood and heart failure.
Often soldiers would break the legs of those hanging on
crosses to speed up
the death.

**gn**

Once the person
reached the crucifixion
site, he would be tied or nailed
through the wrists to the crossbeam.
The crossbeam would then be lifted and tied to the
already upright pole. Pins or a block of wood attached to the pole
provided a seat. The feet were then tied or nailed to the post.

**Jesus predicted His death several times:**
✓ Matthew 16:21; Mark 8:31; Luke 9:22
✓ Matthew 17:22-23; Mark 9:31; Luke 9:44
✓ Matthew 20:18-19; Mark 10:33-34; Luke 18:32-33
✓ John 3:14; 8:28; 12:32-33

Write a prayer thanking God that Jesus
was willing to die on the cross for you.

Dear Heavenly Father,

Ask your parents for a nail.
Attach it here with a piece of
tape as a reminder of what
Jesus did for you.

In Jesus' name, Amen.

# JESUS: RAISED FROM THE DEAD!

RHONDA VANCLEAVE

Jesus did many amazing and wonderful things during the time He was on earth. Crowds of people gathered to hear Him teach and see Him heal the sick and perform other miracles. However, the most important thing Jesus came to do was to be the Savior of the world. When Jesus died, He took the punishment for our sins, but His resurrection proved His power over sin, death, and hell.

Jesus' resurrection and final days on earth included events that are more amazing than Hollywood's best special effects. Imagine a violent earthquake, an angel of the Lord in a bright white robe easily rolling a massive stone away from the tomb entrance, and then sitting on top of the stone! Experienced military guards were so shaken with fear they passed out!

When the chief priests heard about the events, they were afraid of what might happen if the people realized Jesus really was alive. According to Matthew 28:12-13, the chief priests paid some soldiers a large sum of money to spread the lie that Jesus' disciples had stolen His body. However, Jesus was about to provide plenty of proof that He was alive and well!

During the next 40 days, Jesus appeared to lots of people. One time, more than 500 people were there to see Him. Jesus walked, talked, and ate with people. His friends were able to touch Him and know it was really Him and He was alive! Jesus wanted His followers to have no doubt He did everything He ever said He would do.

After 40 days, Jesus promised the disciples the Holy Spirit would soon come to help them. Then, right before their eyes, Jesus ascended (went up) into the clouds. They couldn't take their eyes off the sky. How could Jesus just disappear? Suddenly two men in white clothes appeared and asked the disciples, "Why are you standing here looking up into heaven? Jesus, who has been taken from you, will come back the same way you have seen Him going into heaven."

Jesus came to take the punishment for our sin. He proved He is God. We can trust Him. Isn't it exciting to think that, one day, He will return? He promised. And, Jesus has always kept His promises.

When you realize all the truly amazing things Jesus did, you can't help but want to tell someone! And that's exactly what Jesus wants us to do. The last command Jesus gave His followers (Matthew 28:19-20; Acts 1:8) was to be His witnesses and make disciples!

## DAY 1

### JESUS IS ALIVE!

VERSES OF THE DAY: Matthew 28:1-6
CHALLENGE: Mark 14:28

**DO!** Jesus is no longer dead. He is alive! Can you remember the things the women saw when they went to the tomb?

Use the letters in the box to fill in the blanks. Cross out the letters as you use them.

- An _n_e_ of the L_r_

- The _t_n_ was _o_l_d back

- The angel's appearance was like _i_h_n_n_

  and his _o_e as _h_t_ as _n_w

- The tomb was _m_t_. Jesus was not _h_r_. He

  had been _a_s_d from the _e_d.

- For Jews, the Sabbath begins at sundown on Friday and ends at sundown on Saturday.
- In the New Testament, the Pharisees had strict rules about what could and could not be done on the Sabbath.
- Today, Christians worship on Sunday, the first day of the week—the day of Jesus' resurrection.

**PRAY** Thank God that Jesus is alive! Thank Him for the amazing things He does.

## DAY 2

### GO AND TELL!

VERSES OF THE DAY: Matthew 28:8-10
CHALLENGE: Luke 24:9-12

**DO!** After Jesus appeared to the women, the women hurried to tell the disciples Jesus was alive. The women didn't have cell phones or other quick forms of communication.

If you could text the great news of Jesus' resurrection to someone, to whom would you send the text and what would you say? How do you think he would respond? Write your text conversation here.

- Women were the first eyewitnesses of Jesus' resurrection.
- You can read about this same amazing event in other New Testament books. Check out: Mark 16:1-13; Luke 24:1-12; and John 20:1-18.

**PRAY** Ask God to help you share the good news of the resurrection with your friends like the women who told the disciples.

## PROOF

VERSES OF THE DAY: Matthew 28:16-18; Acts 1:3-4 / CHALLENGE: 1 Corinthians 15:3-11

**DO!** Do the math. A lot of people saw Jesus alive after He was resurrected. Look up each verse and write in the blank the number of people who saw Jesus.

_____ Luke 24:13-15

_____ Luke 24:33-43

_____ John 20:11-16

_____ 1 Corinthians 15:6

_____ 1 Corinthians 15:8

**KNOW!**

✓ After Jesus was resurrected, He did miraculous things and ordinary things to prove He was alive.
  * He walked and talked with people (Luke 24:15-17).
  * He ate with His friends (Luke 24:41-43).
  * He allowed people to touch Him (Luke 24:39).
  * He appeared in a locked room (John 20:19-20).

**PRAY** Thank God for giving us a lot of proof that Jesus is alive.

## PROMISES MADE

VERSES OF THE DAY: Acts 1:4-5,8; Matthew 28:18-20 / CHALLENGE: Matthew 6:31-33

**DO!** After His resurrection, Jesus made some special promises during His last 40 days on earth. The promises give comfort and encouragement to His followers. The "Challenge" verses list some promises Jesus made while He was teaching His followers. Based on the verses you read today, what is your favorite promise? Write it in the space provided.

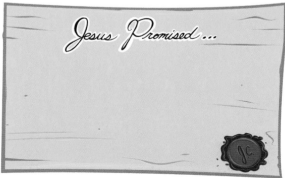

_Jesus Promised ..._

**KNOW!**

✓ Jesus promised the Holy Spirit would be a special helper for believers.
✓ The Holy Spirit can help you know what to say when you talk about God (Mark 13:11; Luke 12:12).
✓ The Holy Spirit is the One who teaches you when you study God's Word (John 14:26).

**PRAY** Thank God for the promises He provided through Jesus. Thank Him for the specific promise you listed.

## DAY 5 — JESUS IS COMING BACK!

VERSES OF THE DAY: Acts 1:9-11
CHALLENGE: John 14:1-3

 When Jesus ascended, the disciples stood gazing into heaven. What did the angels tell the disciples? Write the conversation in the bubbles.

**KNOW!**

✓ The Bible promises Jesus will return one day, but only God knows when that will be (Matthew 24:36).
✓ The Bible says Jesus has all authority in heaven and on earth (Matthew 28:18).
✓ You can use words from a Bible verse when you pray.

**PRAY** Thank God that Jesus "has been given all authority in heaven and on earth."

## DAY 6 — PRAY TOGETHER

VERSES OF THE DAY: Acts 1:12-14
CHALLENGE: Mark 6:3

 Read Acts 1:12-14. The disciples had been with Jesus after His resurrection and saw His miraculous ascension. What did they do next?

Who was there? Put a check mark by the people mentioned in this passage:

___ Peter
___ John
___ Isaiah
___ James
___ Andrew
___ Philip
___ Thomas
___ Abraham

___ Bartholomew
___ Matthew
___ James, son of Alphaeus
___ Noah
___ Simon the Zealot
___ Judas, son of James
___ Mary, mother of Jesus
___ Jesus' brothers

When was the last time you prayed with your family or friends?

**KNOW!**

✓ A "Sabbath-day's journey" described the distance a New Testament Jew was legally allowed to travel on the Sabbath. The distance was about a half of a mile.
✓ Jesus' friends and family members prayed together.
✓ You can pray with family and friends.

**PRAY**  Thank God for your family and friends. Thank Him for hearing you when you pray.

# JESUS: PALM SUNDAY TO EASTER

**Game instructions:**
Locate a game piece for each player, and a coin.

Place game pieces on the "Start" space.

Take turns flipping the coin to determine how many spaces to move:
**Heads = 1 space;**
**Tails = 2 spaces.**

Read the event on each space as you land on it. Find the verses in Matthew 21:1–28:10 that match the space. Follow any directions on the space to move forward or backward before the next player makes his move.

The first person to reach the "Finish" space will shout,
**"Jesus is alive!"**

18. Jesus was raised from the dead (Easter)! Move forward 2 spaces.

**Finish**
Celebrate that Jesus is alive!

17. Jesus was buried in a sealed, guarded tomb.

16. Jesus died.

15. Jesus was crucified between two criminals (Good Friday).

14. Soldiers mocked Jesus.

10. Judas betrayed Jesus with a kiss. Go back 1 space.

13. Crowds shouted, "Crucify Him!" Go back 3 spaces.

12. Jesus was put on trial.

11. Jesus was arrested.

**PARENT PAGE ALERT!**
Invite your parents to play this game with you. As you move your game pieces around the board, work together to find the verses in Matthew 21:1–28:10 that match the spaces. Who will reach the finish space first?

**Start**

1. People praised Jesus as He entered Jerusalem (Palm Sunday).
Move forward 2 spaces.

2. Jesus cleansed the temple complex.

3. Jesus cursed a fig tree.

4. Children praised Jesus.
Move forward 1 space.

5. Jesus told parables and made predictions.

6. A plot was made to kill Jesus.
Move back 2 spaces.

7. Jesus was anointed at Bethany.
Move forward 1 space.

8. Jesus celebrated the Passover with His disciples.

9. Jesus prayed in the garden of Gethsemane.

**NOTE:** You can help the game board lay more flat by laying heavier objects (like books) on the outside edges of your journal. Use coins, different colored paper clips or squares of paper, or other small objects for game pieces.

# THINK ABOUT IT!

Over the last 15 weeks you've learned a lot about the life of Jesus!
Look back through your journal to help you respond to the questions in the boxes below.

**What was your favorite topic to study about Jesus?**

Why?

**What are three things you learned about Jesus you didn't already know?**

1.

2.

3.

**If a friend asked you to describe Jesus' life, what would you tell her?**

Jesus ...

What questions do you still have about Jesus?

Ask your parents, a teacher, or a friend to help you discover the answers to your questions.

What will you do to be a better follower of Jesus?
I will ...

Complete this prayer:

Dear Heavenly Father,

Thank You for sending Jesus ...

In Jesus' name I pray, Amen.

# MY SERMON NOTES

THINGS MY PASTOR SAID:

SOMETHING I LEARNED TODAY:

SOMETHING I CAN DO THIS WEEK RELATED TO THE SERMON:

SOMETHING I CAN TALK WITH MY FAMILY ABOUT:

TODAY'S DATE

TODAY'S SCRIPTURE
READING/SERMON

# MY SERMON NOTES

TODAY'S DATE

TODAY'S SCRIPTURE
READING/SERMON

THINGS MY PASTOR SAID:

SOMETHING I LEARNED TODAY:

SOMETHING I CAN DO THIS WEEK RELATED TO THE SERMON:

SOMETHING I CAN TALK WITH MY FAMILY ABOUT:

# MY SERMON NOTES

TODAY'S DATE

TODAY'S SCRIPTURE
READING/SERMON

THINGS MY PASTOR SAID:

SOMETHING I LEARNED TODAY:

SOMETHING I CAN DO THIS WEEK RELATED TO THE SERMON:

SOMETHING I CAN TALK WITH MY FAMILY ABOUT:

# MY SERMON NOTES

TODAY'S DATE

TODAY'S SCRIPTURE
READING/SERMON

THINGS MY PASTOR SAID:

SOMETHING I LEARNED TODAY:

SOMETHING I CAN DO THIS WEEK RELATED TO THE SERMON:

SOMETHING I CAN TALK WITH MY FAMILY ABOUT:

# MY SERMON NOTES

TODAY'S DATE

TODAY'S SCRIPTURE
READING/SERMON

THINGS MY PASTOR SAID:

SOMETHING I LEARNED TODAY:

SOMETHING I CAN DO THIS WEEK RELATED TO THE SERMON:

SOMETHING I CAN TALK WITH MY FAMILY ABOUT:

# MY SERMON NOTES

TODAY'S DATE

TODAY'S SCRIPTURE
READING/SERMON

THINGS MY PASTOR SAID:

SOMETHING I LEARNED TODAY:

SOMETHING I CAN DO THIS WEEK RELATED TO THE SERMON:

SOMETHING I CAN TALK WITH MY FAMILY ABOUT:

# WHAT COMES NEXT?

## How Do I Keep Growing as a Follower of Jesus?

Congratulations! You completed your *I'm a Christian, Now What? Vol. 2* journal. So now what? On pages 98-99 you wrote things you learned about Jesus as you read the Bible and completed the activities. God wants you to continue learning about Jesus, following Him, and telling other people about Him! Here are some ways you can do that:

☐ Attend Bible study classes at your church.

☐ Participate in worship services.

☐ Read and study your Bible each day.

☐ Pray.

☐ Memorize Bible verses.

☐ Tell your family and friends what you know about Jesus.

☐ Ask questions when you do not understand things.

☐ Talk with people who you know have a close relationship with Jesus.

☐ Read stories about people's relationships with Jesus.

☐ Be open to God doing amazing things in your life.


Can you add some other ways to the list?

☐

☐

☐

# PARENT/CHILD FOLLOW-UP COMMITMENT

Your child has completed the *I'm a Christian, Now What? Vol. 2* journal. Celebrate your child's accomplishment! Although her work in this journal is complete, her journey as a follower of Jesus continues! Here are some suggestions to help your child continue to learn more about Jesus, follow Him, and tell others about Him:

✓ Participate as a family in corporate worship services.

✓ Make it a priority to ensure your child participates regularly in Bible study times.

✓ Be an example for your child of what it means to be a follower of Jesus.

✓ Model Christlike characteristics.

✓ Pray for and with your family on a daily basis.

✓ Seek opportunities for your family to minister and serve your church, community, and the world.

✓ Accept your God-given responsibility to nurture your child.

✓ Provide additional resources for your child to grow in his spiritual life.

✓ Ensure what your child learns is true biblical teaching.

You and your child began this journal by making a pledge to one another. End this journal the same way by completing the pledges below.

## PARENT'S PLEDGE

☐ I promise to continue praying for and encouraging you each day.

☐ I promise to live my life in a way that will provide a positive example for you to learn from.

☐ I promise to help you grow as a follower of Jesus by participating in regular worship times as a family and with our church family.

☐ I promise to allow God to work in your life as He sees best (not as I see best).

☐ I promise to support and encourage you as you grow in your relationship with Jesus.

_____     _____
Parent's Signature                                          Date

## CHILD'S PLEDGE

☐ I promise to continue learning what it means to be a follower of Jesus.

☐ I promise to seek to obey you and follow God's plan for our family.

☐ I promise to pray each day.

☐ I promise to allow God to work in my life as He sees best.

☐ I promise to talk with you and ask questions about following Jesus.

_____     _____
Child's Signature                                            Date

# MEET THE WRITERS

All of us writers for *I'm a Christian, Now What? Vol. 2* are very happy about the opportunity we were given to help you grow in your relationship with God. Even as we wrote, we prayed that kids like you would learn more about Jesus and what it means to follow Him. Thanks for letting us help you grow as a Christian!

Favorite animal: cheetah

Favorite pizza toppings: pepperoni, black olives, and extra cheese

Gordon's dream vacation: climb Machu Picchu

Gordon Brown

Favorite foods: Mexican and Chinese, but not eaten together!

Favorite subject in school: history

Weirdest food Todd ever ate: fried chicken's feet in Hong Kong

Todd Capps

Favorite hobby: drinking coffee

Favorite pizza topping: mushrooms

Henry's dream vacation: travel across Europe and visit historic sites

Henry Dutton

Favorite ice cream flavor: chocolate with chocolate syrup topped with chocolate chips and pecans

Favorite color: blue

Where Carol squeezes a tube of toothpaste: in the middle!

Carol Ellis

Favorite food: mac and cheese

Favorite school subject: music

If Bill were to perform in a circus he would be: a clown. He loves to make people laugh!

Bill Emeott

Favorite hobby: playing tug-of-war with Ranger, his Rat Terrier

Favorite Bible story: God rescues Peter from prison

Favorite holiday: the one Landry is celebrating at the moment

Landry Holmes

Favorite candy:
Haribo® raspberries

Favorite hobby:
gardening/yard
work

Animal Jeff would
choose to be: a
giraffe, so he could
see everything
because of his
height

Jeff Land

Favorite part of the
day: bedtime

Favorite book
of the Bible:
Deuteronomy

Color Tim would be
in a box of crayons:
burnt sienna
(because the name
is cool!)

Tim Pollard

Favorite hobby:
pottery

Favorite animal:
moose

Weirdest food
Tracey ever ate:
moose tartare and
freshwater eel

Tracey Rogers

Favorite color:
anything bright!

Favorite food:
brownies

Weirdest food Klista
has eaten: escargot
("yuck!")

Klista Storts

Favorite ice cream
flavor: chocolate
chip cookie dough

Favorite book of
the Bible: Hebrews

If William were
to perform in a
circus he would be:
the ringmaster, so
he could build the
drama and tell a
few jokes!

William Summey

Favorite color:
PURPLE!

Favorite candy:
Three Musketeers®
candy bar

Time of day Rhonda
is most silly:
2-4 p.m.

Rhonda VanCleave

Favorite school
subject: English

Favorite food:
Tex Mex

Color Jerry would
be in a box of
crayons: green
(because he was
born on
St. Patrick's Day)

Jerry Vogel

# ABOUT ME!

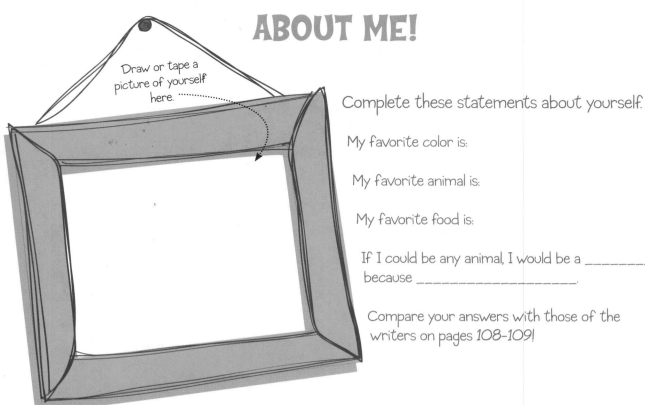

Draw or tape a picture of yourself here.

Complete these statements about yourself.

My favorite color is:

My favorite animal is:

My favorite food is:

If I could be any animal, I would be a _____ because _____.

Compare your answers with those of the writers on pages 108-109!

## Here are some other GREAT Resources!

*I'm a Christian, Now What? Volume 1* (005490151)

*Holman Illustrated Bible Dictionary for Kids* (005268545)

## Check out these devotional magazines at www.lifeway.com/kids.

This certificate is awarded to

_____

on _____
(Date)

For completing the
I'm A Christian, Now What? Volume 2 Journal

_____
(Parent's Signature)